A Patriot's Letters To AMERICA

Daniel Harmeson

A Patriot's Letters To America
Copyright © 2021 by Daniel Harmeson

All rights reserved. No part of this publication may be reproduced, distributed, or transmitted in any form or by any means, including photocopying, recording, or other electronic or mechanical methods, without the prior written permission of the publisher or author, except in the case of brief quotations embodied in critical reviews and certain other noncommercial uses permitted by copyright law.

Although every precaution has been taken to verify the accuracy of the information contained herein, the author and publisher assume no responsibility for any errors or omissions. No liability is assumed for damages that may result from the use of information contained within.

Library of Congress Control Number: 2020925224
ISBN-13:   Paperback: 978-1-64749-317-2
           ePub: 978-1-64749-318-9

Printed in the United States of America

GoToPublish LLC
1-888-337-1724
www.gotopublish.com
info@gotopublish.com

"Down through history, there have been many revolutions, but virtually all of them only exchanged one set of rulers for another set of rulers. Ours was the only truly philosophical revolution. It declared that government would have only those powers granted to it by the People".

Ronald Reagan

"I don't believe in the Constitution because I'm American. I'm American because I believe in the Constitution".

J. S. B. Morse.

"Patriotism is not short frenzied out burst of emotion, but the tranquil and steady dedication of a lifetime".

Adlai Stevenson

OPENING STATEMENT.

I learned many years ago that a coin has two sides for a reason. Each side is different but just as important to the overall coin. Both sides should be looked at and evaluated. It takes both sides to make a coin. Much like our political system. The two major parties, Democrat and Republican. Not discounting the Conservatives Libertarians or Independents. They are the parties that add compromise in my opinion. Our country needs this diversity in politics to bring ideas together to serve all. It takes all sides. I speak often in my letters of compromise, critical thinking and extreme ownership. Those elements are crucial for this Republic to succeed. Years ago I used to lean Democrat but switched to Republican. No big deal. I used to hear of Democrats voting Republican and vice versa. Still happens today, to some extent. But in our Republic these days it appears the Dems have strayed too far from what they once were. This transformation they speak of doesn't seem to make the coin whole. It appears they want both sides of the coin to be the same, one party/ Government rule. Somehow that doesn't register with me. I am all for diversity, inclusion and tolerance. This hatred for one man has blinded them. The hatred of America by a group of citizens is alarming. It should not be about one person, rather about America. It is about Our Republic, our country. About the Constitution, The Declaration of Independence and the Bill of Rights.

Through these letters one might get the impression I am a hard liner. I am an American who wants this country to remain America under the framework of our founding Fathers. That being said, I will not accept the take over and transformation of this Republic. Make it better. Improve this Republic. Don't steal it. I will support compromise, but I ain't hearing or seeing compromise lately. I am a Patriot. I stand for America, the American idea and this experiment in human freedoms. I will not waiver on that. I have been to countries that do not have what We the People have. Each of us should cherish these freedoms and build on them for our children, our grandchildren and so on. No country on earth has what we have. It ain't perfect. It ain't easy. But it sure as heck beats being controlled by the Government. I believe in the Bill of Rights, the Declaration of Independence and the Constitution as it is written today. These documents are the heart and soul of this country. We the People are the body of this country. And our freedoms are the heartbeat of this country. Not the word salads of career politicians who seek power. We the People will make and keep this America getting better. The both sides of the coin I am talking about is the American coin. I will not compromise my love of America. I believe in the American Dream. I have lived the American Dream. I believe to wish is to dream. To dream is to will. And to will is to fulfill the dream. We, Americans, have the Right to Pursue Happiness. In closing I say to every American, believers and non believers, start pursuing happiness, wish, dream and will. Stop relying on others and the Government to fulfill your dreams. Fulfill your own dreams, it's a lot more satisfying. God Bless America and God Bless Americans.

Dear America,

I have known you my whole life. I have become you, America. You are the reason as a child I ran freely and played in the woods, swam in the rivers, walked through the corn fields, fished in the ponds, dreamt of being a soldier and dying for my men and my country. I did this worry free. Free being the optimum word. Bonded by a common cause, love of country, love of Freedoms, love of Liberties and love of our way of life. Now I cling to those memories. I fear that our Republic has no common beliefs. No love of the common good. No love of you, America. Without that we are not a Republic. There are those who wish to control our grammar. Our religious beliefs. Erase our history. For what? Power? Transformation? Without all those beliefs we are nothing. There are those who want to transform this Republic for no common good or common bond. We will become nothing. A wandering conglomerate of individuals roaming this land for no common reason or cause. Ruled by elitists who want only power and control. And the sad thing is, many of your people cannot connect the dots. We will become a country of anarchy. Controlled by morons in power and thugs in the streets. Without a history, America never existed. We never existed. Writing this aches my heart and fuels my love for you, America. How can I abandon you? You raised me, you were with me when I served 27 years in the military under an Oath to support and defend. You influenced me on how to raise my children and teach my grandchildren. You are the one my wife, an immigrant who became an American, fell in love with and is so grateful for the opportunities afforded her. You never abandoned us, when others despised and cursed you. For that I have given you my never ending support and will never abandon you. So help me God. How can I stop this Republic, which our founders knew was fragile, from becoming a soulless land of wanderers always wanting and never caring for a common united cause? We the People need to rise up and keep you, America, alive and on track to seeking a more perfect Union.

Always loyal and faithful.

v/r
Dan

Dear America,

　　A Patriots Pledge:
- We will not forsake you America.
- We will not surrender to tyranny or relinquish our American rights.
- We will support and defend the Constitution of the United States of America against all enemies foriegn and domestic.
- We will not burn or loot stores.
- We will not disobey police.
- We will not assault those who wear hats that bear names of those we do not agree with.
- We will not destroy other people's property.
- We will not come to your neighborhood and rant curse words and tell you we are taking your property.
- We will not tear down gates to private property and threaten to burn your house.
- We will not block an entrance to a hospital and chant " We hope you die."
- We will not burn a Federal building or police station.
- We will not destroy statues.
- We will protect our family and friends.
- We will not forget our history. We stand for America, Freedom and Liberty for all American citizens.
- We will defend America peacefully with our words, our votes, and assembly. We are Americans. We are reasonable and God fearing people who will remain relentless to maintain our Freedoms and Liberties. God Bless America.

Always faithful and loyal.

　　v/r
　　Dan

Dear America,

I have come across this sobering quote from September 29, 1959. I want to share it with you.

Russia's Krushchev delivered this speech:

"Your children's children will live under communism. You Americans are so gullible. No, you won't accept communism outright; but we will keep feeding you small doses of socialism until you will finally wake up and find you already have Communism. We will not have to fight you; We will so weaken your economy, until you fall like overripe fruit into our hands. The democracy will cease to exist when you take away from those who are willing to work and give to those who would not."

Remember this: Socialism leads to Communism. I believe socialism is the financial platform from which Communism springs from.

These are the eight levels of controls by Saul Alinsky to transform a nation through socialism into communism.

1. Health care: control health care and you control the people.
2. Poverty: Increase the poverty level as high as possible, poor people are easier to control and will not fight back if you are providing everything for them.
3. Debt: Increase the debt to an unattainable level. That way you are able to increase taxes and this will produce more poverty.
4. Gun Control: Remove the ability to defend themselves from the Government. That way you are able to create a police state.
5. Welfare: Take control of every aspect, food, housing and income of their lives because that will make them fully dependent on the government.
6. Education: Take control of what people read and listen to. Take control of what children learn in school.
7. Religion: Remove the belief in God from the government and schools. Because people need to believe in only the government knowing what is best for them.

8. Class Warfare: Divide the People into the wealthy and the poor. Eliminate the middle class. This will cause more discontent and it will be easier to tax the wealthy with the support of the poor.

America, this is what is happening today. Our framers put together documents to stop this. But those documents are being ignored. Especially the Constitution. The Leftists want to change the Constitution, the body. They could care less about the Declaration, the soul. It is happening now. Has been happening incrementally for over 50 years and so many are naive. Education was the key to this wave of thinking. Socialism/Communism has never worked in any country and our youth now believe it is Utopia. Hook line and sinker. They swallowed it and are now marching forward. The remaining Americans must rise and stop this. We need your help. Help us help ourselves.

Always loyal and forever faithful.

    v/ r
    Dan

Dear America,

The American Flag. For one moment can you imagine what the Colonials felt carrying it into battle against King George III's Army and his tyrannical rule? Or, the feeling of our brave men in Iwo Jima when it was raised? Or each and everyday, all across this world Military men and women raise it, salute it and honor it each morning and evening? Or, how it feels to see a casket cloaked with it as a fallen soldier is transported home after paying the ultimate price for America? I know that feeling. The pain and pride all bunched together. The final bond with Ole Glory. What is the Fourth of July? And, what does it mean today? What does our Flag mean today? America, an ideal, an experiment in human freedom/liberty. Are we to abandon that ideal/experiment over rough times? That is not what the American Flag stands for. We fight for freedom, liberty and justice for all. Is it hard? Yes. The only easy day was yesterday. Our Flag is a symbol of hard work, sacrifice, mistakes and Freedom. Honor it in your own way this July 4th. I only hope there are enough Americans who believe, who will fight for it, honor it, and remember the sacrifices made for it. Don't give up on this ideal/experiment. Fly the Flag. And let's keep America improving by learning from the past, celebrating its progress and not repeating past mistakes. The goal is not to erase the past but learn from it. Respect the Flag, love the freedoms/liberties, maintain the Republic and be the Country everyone wants to be a part of. We are Americans. A Republic. One Nation. An ideal. An experiment in human freedom/ liberties. Our symbol is "The Flag."

Always faithful and loyal.

v/r
Dan

Dear America,

As I watch our politicians exploit the unfortunate situations of 2 black men killed by police officers, both victims were criminals for the most part, and then be hailed as heroes. I cringe at how low the Dems will go. I will be one of the first to say that both policemen exercised extremely poor judgement and a lack of situational control. That is one area the police, in my humble opinion, need extensive training. For the Democrats nominee for Vice President to say she was proud of the latest black man who was shot by a policeman. It's just ridiculous. Pure, 100% political pandering. Proud that a man who resisted arrest and attacked police officers to the point of being shot. He had a violent sexual assault against a woman and was not suppose to be in that area. That is why the police were there to arrest him. So much for the Dems being for the sexually assaulted victims. Especially women. The Dems have no shame. What about the almost 60 black children shot this year? Where is BLM and their Marxist's ways to eradicate capitalism? Where are the Dems and their holier than thou BS? Criminals become heroes and children become targets of drive by shooting. Neighborhoods become war zones where people lose their businesses. For what? To make a statement? What statement? I cannot believe there are so many shallow thinking people in this Republic who cannot see through the smoke screen. I am so sorry America, that so many are that naive and misinformed. The problem, in my humble opinion, is the failed programs of our so called leaders. And their greed for power at all costs. They have transformed into what our Founding Fathers tried to guard us against. Most citizens are just ignorant to what the Framers tried to accomplish. Pure ignorance exploited by evil politicians and a news media that is just as evil. A Democratic nominee for President is lying to the cameras about a sitting President to win favor with his base. Does he not think or remember there are videos of his past comments? What a worthless suit and shallow man he is. We the People see through the smoke and mirrors. I have grandchildren who are smarter and more honest than this man. They have more integrity than most politicians. I could go on and on how this Democratic nominee has lied, back tracked on statements, or regurgitated thoughts from others. He is almost always looking in the rear view mirror and criticizing others. Ain't hard to do that. Da! And the real kicker is that the Democratic nominee for President blames the now President for tens of thousands of COVID deaths for lack of action against this horrible virus. When he did not agree early on what the President was doing to shut down travel. It's all for theatrics and show. I believe in my heart of hearts that the Democratic nominee for President is so out of touch with real Americans that it baffles me to the point of how can this cynical man take the helm of this great Republic. The Dems have poisoned our youth through education for over 60 years and created an ignorant and angry culture. The Transformation is in full force and the current President wants to keep America and Americans first. Our current President loves you America. The Democratic nominees for President and Vice President in my opinion, do not truly love America. The Dems are pure politicians who are heartless and don't really give a damn about any of us Americans. They only care about themselves. Take heed America. You are being duped by evil soulless individuals. May God help the Americans who actually love this country. And may God forgive those Americans who have lost their way.

Always faithful and loyal.

    v/r
    Dan

Dear America,

I must tell you of my wife's love for you. She is an amazing woman. Born into poverty. One of 13 children. Raised in a country thousands of miles from your shores. Growing up in a world of self preservation, having to work hard and live off the land. Education was a luxury and came second to surviving. Somehow she survived, got a job , we met, and got married. Had children. And now have grandchildren. The Great American Dream. My wife entered America legally. Went through all the paperwork. Medical screening. Interviews. Visits to the embassy for entry interviews. And was given a document to become a legal immigrant. Within a few short years she became a United States citizen. I remember her swearing in ceremony. After swearing in she was given a small flag, which she still displays today, 34 years later. She believes and embraces the American way and celebrates freedom everyday. Displays Ole Glory all year long. Total assimilation without forgetting her heritage. She is a true role model for all who want to immigrate and assimilate into the Republic legally. She is an American and proud of it. Now that is a real feel good American story. Go America!

Always loyal and faithful.

    v/r
    Dan

Dear America,

It pains me to see what we have become as a Republic. Hurts so deep that my very soul screams for it to stop. I now know the hurt you have felt all these years when unapologetic morons spit, stomped, urinated and burned on your flag America. It rocks me to the point of uncontrollable disgust. I was born and raised around Democrats. Strong union town. Moderate for the most part. I began to see the evil of the Democrats in the late 60's. My neighborhood was a low to middle income community who were mostly democrats and union workers. My parents raised me and my sisters to accept all people regardless of color. So, I watched, listened and studied Democrats for many years. In the mid to early 80's I began watching and listening to the Republican Party. Then came President Regan. I was convinced then that Democrats had no real meaningful agenda. I had witnessed what the Dems would say and do. I converted to Republican and have not looked back since. So, when I come across hard in my letters on the Dems, it is because I was surrounded by them. I know the evil in their hearts. Today's Dems are much different. More evil. How can they sleep at night knowing that almost everything they do and say is such crap? Look at what the Democratic nominee did the other day. Prostrated himself to the father of a criminal who was shot by police for resisting arrest. For the record, I do not think the police officer who shot the person was right. He screwed up. Panicked and made a horrible decision. Policemen need better training. That will be the subject of another letter. Back on subject. So this act just to gain some votes is so wrong on many levels. This father allegedly has written bile statements on social media and favors a known anti Semitic person. Have the Dems no shame? They definitely have no scruples. They say and do anything to gain power. Now you know some of the reasons I left them. Hell they were the most racist people in my neighborhood. But they are the first to call others racists. Remember when I told you I was taught that a liar will almost always call you a liar first just to shift blame. Consider this America. The Dems are the ones supporting the violent protests across America. Fact: The Dems have not tried to stop it. Hell they haven't even come out, until recently, and said boo. And the only reason they said something now, which wasn't much, was because their Democratic nominee was slipping in the polls. How lame is that? They are more evil than you can imagine. Let's sum it up shall we. The Dems hate you, America and want to transform you. The Dems play the race card just to divide Americans. Not saying racism does exist because it does. The Dems are so far left that Socialism/communism is their agenda. The Dems have created identity politics which puts people in boxes. The Dems trample all over the Constitution and ignore the Declaration of Independence/ Bill of rights. The Dems want to defund the police and have launched a campaign to discredit and demonize the police. The Dems are supporting Marxist's groups who want to dismantle capitalism, and will have to repay them by cowering to their wishes. Or suffer the consequences. The Dems are weaponizing COVID 19 for political gain and instilling a culture of obedience and control. And destroying the economy of this Republic to win an election. The Dems want big government and control over the economy so they can control our lives. The Dems leadership is clustered with Anti American values and are heartless unpatriotic morons who think they need to control We the People. I see it. Have seen it. And only hope rational people see it. The Dems are all in on this election and will do anything to win. I mean anything. If they lose there will be no second chance. They have exposed themselves for what they really are. Only a blind moron could not see it. They will bring destruction and death to you, America. I believe that with every fiber in my body. They must not win this election. Our Nation. Our Republic. Our freedoms/liberties are at stake. Our very way of life will change. Chaos will come to our door and this Republic will fall. But rest assure America, I will not forsake or abandon you. I stand with you no matter how terrible it may get. No matter the outcome of this election. You will be our shining light. Our beacon to freedom/liberties. Our resolve to ensure Life, Liberties and Freedom will live on. Your Flag will be our symbol. I will never surrender to Socialism/Communism, transformation of the American Dream, or the American way of life. This experiment in human freedom and the American ideal will live on in me until my last breath. So help me God.

Always faithful and loyal.

    v/r
    Dan

Dear America,

Can't believe this one. In Washington DC, a couple of Pro Life Supporters were arrested for writing in chalk on a sidewalk in front of a Planned Parenthood facility. They wrote "Pre-born Black Lives Matter." The Mayor had decreed it ok to paint on the street for BLM, but obviously only if you supported their political views and Pro abortion. People are using paint and fire to deface or destroy property. Even writing foul language and threats are ok. But chalk on a sidewalk is an arresting offense? And it was in support for unborn black children. I guess BLM means something very different to different people. Maybe everyone should read the BLM mission statement. How hypocritical is this? Can't begin to understand the evil mindset some possess. This and other actions only further support the theory that the BLM agenda is not what the average person thinks it is. It is a Marxist's movement cloaked in gaining support for Black people and equality, but is entirely something different. Only certain Black folk matter. When will the madness end? Am I alone on an island and losing my mind? Or have " We the People" been rope-a-doped? I am all for equality and recognizing each person as a member of the human race, and strongly support positive change in creating a more perfect Union. An American Union. But this country is so divided and will not commit to compromise. Or intelligent dialogue. I fear this Republic is on the verge of catastrophic collapse. Politicians and biased media are partially to blame. We the People are also partially to blame. Yes, we are. We the People have allowed our elected officials to run amuck. Blind to the storm brewing. All concerned should be alarmed. And be prepared to pay the consequences if the radical left gains the power. I ask each of your citizens, America, this. If you really care for America what will you do? Turn a blind eye? Vote party line? Or vote for America and the freedoms and liberties drafted in the Constitution and Declaration of Independence? Will you accept the type of behavior and civil unrest being displayed on the streets as the new norm? Will you not stop the radical movement towards socialism/communism that is heading your way? The bigger question is, are you in favor of total transformation and totalitarian government that could gain the power in this republic? Ponder that then let your conscience be your guide. If the voters decide to turn hard left, then let the chips fall where they may. And hope for the best. I wish I had cheerier news, but these are worrisome times.

Always faithful and loyal.

    v/ r
    Dan

Dear America,

Imagine a world that was so perfect in every way. All inhabitants were happy, cordial, possessed no bias, no prejudice, expressed no hatred toward others, felt safe, wanted for nothing, everything was provided for them, no crime, everyone had a job and was paid the same, and the Government ensured all of this. Okay, wake up. That utopia will never exist. Not in a society where humans live. Not in a society where activists stoke the fire and keep us mere humans rattled and wanting for stuff. Not in a society where each individual doesn't believe that it is their responsibility to make their own way in life. Not in a society where there are those who have everything and there are those who want everything but don't have the means to get it and will not work hard to get everything. Not in a society where humans feel entitled and want to cancel stuff that they feel is offensive. Not in a society that is unwilling to compromise and accept a happy median. Not in a society where there are more who want than there are willing to work. Not in a society that does not believe in its Constitution and Declaration of Independence. Not in a society where many hate the country they live in. Not in a society that has no respect for law and order. The playing field will never be level. Never. All we can do as a Nation is ensure all are equal in the pursuit of happiness, have access to a good and fair education, create an environment of equal justice, learn to compromise through civil dialogue and treat everyone with respect. Accept or at least acknowledge the idea that a sovereign Nation is in the best interest of the Nation. Maintain a viable and well trained military to protect the Nation. Learn to accept the fact that there will always be those who have more. Spend more time bettering yourself than fretting over those who have more. At least each individual has the right to pursue their dream. There will always be greed and those who want the power. And will do or say anything to achieve it or keep it. Believe in, We The People, have the power as outlined in the framework of our Constitution and Declaration of Independence to shut down tyranny and maintain our Nation's Governance under those documents. This Nation was not founded or framed to have big Government. But rather to give the people the power. Our current politicians have it backwards. This experiment in freedoms and liberties is still growing. There is no chance ever that 350 million people will ever be satisfied all the time. Ask yourself this question. Do you believe in America? If the answer is yes. Then work to keep America and build on the founding Fathers' documents and make it better. Enjoy the freedoms and liberties. Reject big Government. Take responsibility for your actions and your pursuit of the American Dream and accept the outcome. If the answer is no. Simply leave and find a country that fits your version of how you want to live. Do not take Real Americans' lives in this Republic away from them just because you don't like it. For I believe there are enough Real Americans who want to keep this life and strive to improve on this way of life. God Bless America.

Always faithful and loyal.

    v/ r
    Dan

Dear America,

As we approach July 4th, a time of great celebration, once again you are under attack. This time from within. An attack to transform you and quite possibly erase the American dream has been waged. Not the first time you have had to endure adversity or threat of ending this American Ideal. This experiment in human freedom. This threat is different. One of globalism, cultural revolution and highly political. A Marxist's takeover is brewing. The total dismantling of the American Dream. The greatest power grab of your existence is about to unfold. Total control by our Government is the end game. How can we help you? You have endured so much and yet delivered so much. I feel we have failed you, as citizens of the Greatest Country to ever have come to fruition. Although, as a Republic, we have made great strides to overcome the ways of the past and move past those sins. It has proven to never be enough. For over 50 years some of our citizens, elected officials and educators have made it their mission to transform this Republic into a global Socialists/Communists nation. Why do they do this to you? There is never enough of progressing, nothing good enough, no amount of making right the wrongs to satisfy them. This movement is determined to bring you down. I apologize for the multitudes of misinformed, misdirected, brainwashed self centered, shallow thinking individuals, and for those who strive to abolish Patriotism. How do we stop this movement to change you, America, the Land of the free, the Home of the brave? How can we save the belief in The Constitution and Declaration of Independence? How can we save you? There is always a way. As Americans, the ones who still believe, we must find a way to work this out through compromise and stability within the citizenry. I will write to you again soon. Until then, America, believe in us Americans, as we will find a way to save this Republic, maintain our freedoms and liberties. Forever grateful. I will stand by You, support You, and defend You.

Always faithful and loyal.

    v/r
    Dan

Dear America,

Happy birthday America.

Today is a day of celebrating our Independence, enjoying family, friends, relaxing, Bar-B-Qing and having a few cold ones. And of course shooting off fireworks. A fun filled day. We fished for our supper from our pond and enjoyed the wooded scenery that surrounds us. The grandkids ran around playing and soaked in the great outdoors. Freedom and liberties have afforded us this moment. We owe you many thanks America.

- Thank you for the Constitution, the body of our Republic.
- Thank you for the Declaration of Independence, the soul of our Republic.
- Thank you for the opportunity to serve you for 27 years. And take the Oath to solemnly swear to support and defend the Constitution of the United States of America , against all enemies foreign and domestic. Domestic being important in today's environment. An oath I will continue to uphold. So help me God.
- Thank you for paving the way through our Republic's framework for my lovely wife to immigrate, assimilate and become an American citizen, legally. I can assure you my wife is a flag flying American. I am so proud of her.
- Thank you for the Pursuit of Happiness. Both my wife and I come from low income families and have worked hard. We were not privileged. Just Blessed. We made our own bones. Raised two great children who have provided us with four beautiful grandchildren. We want them to live the American Dream, work hard, expect nothing from our government, and make their own life in a Free Republic, with all the liberties. We are truly blessed. God Bless You America.
- Thank you for all our brave men and women who have paid the ultimate price serving and defending You. Please honor them. We do.

- Thank you for persevering through all the rough times and challenges thrown at you.
- Thank you for the founding Fathers' foresight to draft the Constitution and Declaration in such a way that included checks and balances. Their vision created the American ideal and framed this human experiment in freedom. I only hope we can keep the torch burning.
- Thank you for creating an environment where Americans became one of the most gracious countries in the world. A country who became the World's police force who helped overcome Socialists/Communists aggression. I hope we can overcome the Socialists/Communists surge coming our way.
- Thank you for the Right to bear arms.
- Thank you for our framers' critical thinking process. A process not being taught or encouraged now. Let's hope there are enough people who engage in this process and actively use it.
- Thank you for being you. Weathered and toughened by time and trials. Wisened by mistakes. Tested. Tried. And true.

Forever loyal and faithful.

    v/r
    Dan

Dear America,

A storm is brewing, and you are the center of the vortex. What is at stake is the American way of life. You America may be just a distant thought in the minds of many come this November. We the People may not celebrate your birthday as a National Holiday next year. Ponder that for a moment. The politics in this day and age is evil and divisive. Even the Supreme Court has become a political arena. The difference between our two candidates running for President is: One is for America first. One is for America last. One fights for the American worker. One fights for Socialists/ Communists radical ideals and will fold like a wet Navy blanket if challenged. One loves America. One wants to transform America. One is a first time politician. One has been in politics for 40 plus years and supported failed programs. Now he has the answers. One makes promises and keeps them. One promises free stuff and less liberties. One supports the Second Amendment. One wants to take Americans' weapons. One wants and has given tax cuts. One wants to raise taxes. One wants to ease regulations on small businesses. One wants to choke small businesses with regulations. One wants law and order. One actually supports defunding and diminishing law and order while supporting a Marxist's group. One understands how to negotiate for the betterment of Americans. One only understands how to exploit the power of being an elected official to better oneself and keep party power. One came into office rich. One got rich from being an elected official. One works for only one dollar. One takes every penny and wants more. One gave up the chance to become richer. One only wants to become richer. One is like us, We the People. One thinks he is above We the People and we need his advice to just exist. One is under constant attack by the media. One gets softball questions and can do no wrong. One does not use his power to destroy others. One has been part of an attack by the Deep State to destroy an individual. One knows he works for We the People. One thinks he dictates to We the People. One wants to lift the American spirit and encourage us to live the American Dream. One wants to crush the American Dream and make us obedient to the new world order. One wants to create new jobs and bring jobs back to America. One wants to create dependency on the government and let other countries take our jobs. One wants Americans to rise out of poverty and succeed. One wants to take more money from Americans pockets to fund radical agendas. One is a self made person. One is a government made person. One wants smaller government and Americans to be free to make choices. One wants the government to make choices for Americans because Americans cannot make their own choices. One is strong, marches to his own drum and is not afraid. One is weak and follows the crowd. I could go on and on. Tough decision here. Da. I'll go for the one who believes in America first.

Always loyal, faithful and always 100% American.

   v/r
   Dan

Dear America,

    I wrote to you previously on July 9, 2020, about a storm brewing. I was wrong. The storm is here. Has been here. I missed that. My bad. I should know better. Won't happen again. I will remain on a higher alert. The Silent majority who love and support you, where are they? Do they still exist? Why are they remaining silent? Are they afraid to speak out? Organize? Afraid of the criticism or retaliation from radical marxists? Afraid they will lose their job? Or think all that is going on is a fad? Maybe they don't understand, are not paying attention, have not studied the situation, or just don't care. Whatever the reason for not speaking out, the silent majority is aiding and abetting to the destruction of this Great Republic. I hope they are ready to accept the fact that the Democrats are no longer regular Democrats. The Democratic Party is now the party of Socialist/Communist. The transformation is being played out per the Marxists play book and those moderate Democrats don't or won't accept it. Or maybe they are just ignorant to the situation at hand. How can they be so naive? Not one Democratic politician has said boo and even the Ex Vice President running for President, has not said anything about the violence in some of your bigger, Democratic run cities. They, the Dems, want this to continue. Again, right out of the Marxist playbook. Refer to my letter dated 8 July, 2020 where I shared an excerpt from a September 29, 1959 speech from Russia's Khrushchev about America becoming Communist, and the 8 steps to Socialism/communism. The Kraken has been released. And the sad thing is they, the Dems, think they can put it back in the bottle. News flash. Won't happen unless you bow to the radical demands to destroy this Republic. Politicians never get it. Power is their goal at all expense. The violence going on in some of these cities is being under reported. They, the Dems, do not want it to get widespread attention. They want to abolish you, America. Again that is the end game. And to those who do not see it, the deception, the art of propaganda, the demonization of law enforcement and abolishment of this country. I say this, " If you support this action to destroy America, then You have made your choice, turned your back on America, stepped into that world, and will get what comes your way". I don't say this lightly. I have family members who will vote for this Democratic incompetent nominee for President and his radical party. The Kraken will remain loose and nothing good will result. You are either for America or you are not. The line is drawn in the sand. Maybe all police should just walk off the job and let the chips lie where they fall. Maybe all investors should stop investing and everyone pull their money out of every bank and 401k. Maybe all the so called peaceful protestors destroying property and attacking those who think differently should be allowed to continue without interference. How about all American citizens just give up their freedoms and liberties to the so called holier than thou politicians who support Socialism/Communism and become good little commies who want the government to tell them how to live their lives. I say, Bullshit! I can compromise. But I will not stand by quietly while there is a movement to destroy you, America. I will support you America without regret. Organizing the silent and not so silent majority to save this Experiment in Human Freedom and American Ideal is paramount. We need the real "We the People" to take a stand and save you, America. Loud, peaceful voices and lots of votes.

Always faithful and loyal.

   v/r
   Dan

Dear America,

Sorry to bother you so late. Remember that storm I keep saying is brewing in your Republic. It's here. All the cards are on the table now. Every true blooded American who is concerned over the Transformation of you America, should be worried. Hells bells they should be scared. I have had co-workers come up to me and voice their concern over the fate of your Republic. What can I tell them? It's okay. Things will turn out just fine. Just vote and the radical Left's push to change you, America, will go away. You and I know that is not true. The violence in our cities will not stop. It will get worse. Mobocracy is here in full force. They have momentum and appear to have a taste for it. The Dems nominee for President has made a pact with a Democratic/Socialist Senator. A 110 page, plus or minus, manifesto. He even said he would be the most Progressive President in history. That is code speak for Socialism communism. And the Squad, four Elected Socialists, as they are called, actually they are just a four person fire team. A squad is 13. Sorry, military speak. They have been quiet as has the Democratic/Socialists. Until today. Why I ask? They were laying low and maybe did not want to bring attention to the real deal awaiting We the People the last few days before the election. But something happened that changed the dynamics of the election. RBG passed away. Oh, sorry. A very famous Supreme Court Justice who leaned left. I actually liked her. Brave, smart and a fighter. God rest her soul. But now the Dems are worried over the fact that the President will nominate a replacement. They are unhinged. Actually they do not want the President to nominate a replacement until after the election. All kinds of goobly-gok is coming from the Dems. Bottom line. It's all about power. Power. Power and more power. Nothing is off the table now. Impeachment. They even say the Republicans have no right to put another Justice on the court before an election. Even though the Constitution is clear on this. The President has the Constitutional right to nominate a replacement. The Senate has the right to vote and act. The threat of more violence, burning of buildings and more riots have already been made. Threats to harass Senators to place fear and to intimidate has already been deployed. And now the elected Socialists who have been relatively quiet are opening up. That means the Democrats are worried. The Supreme Court is now 8. Should be 9. What happens if the Supreme Court is needed to determine the outcome of the upcoming election. I cannot even begin to tell you about all the BS spewing from the mouths of some of your elected officials. Outrageous. I know, I am rambling again. Collect thoughts. This election is electrifying, and now it has become even more so. I cannot remember when more had been at stake in a Presidential election than now. The table is set. Pro-American or Socialists/communists. That's the way I see it. And I am not alone. What other conclusion are we to determine? You should see the posturing from the Dems. Scheming and plotting the next move. I hope the Republicans stand tall and do the right thing. Cause the Dems sure as hell would do it. President Trump showed them how to fight. Look I am all for working together and compromising, but that ship has sailed and won't be back to port anytime soon. Yes, I know there are two sides to a coin. But one side wants to reinvent the other side to change the coin forever. And I happen to believe in the coin and don't want it to change. I want it to get better. And it won't get better under this environment. You must remain America. And we must get better as Americans. We the People must quell this radical storm and calm the waters so we can build on what The Framers wanted the Republic to be. Okay, it's getting late and We the People got work to do to save this American ideal, this experiment in human freedoms and the American Dream.

Always faithful and loyal.

> v/r
> Dan

Dear America,

Today I passed through Phoenix Airport and witnessed a Marine Color Guard off loading a Flag draped casket from an airplane. Then load it into a hearse. It was a scene I thought I would not see again. The final bound of an American warrior with your/our American Flag. I was proud to see so many stop and pay their respects from inside the airport. Outside there were 4 fire trucks lined up and one flew Ole Glory. There were police cars with flashers on. So many working on the tarmac lined up to pay respect. Family and friends of our fallen Marine were there as the Marine on his journey home came off the plane. It was touching to witness the visible grief, the prayers being said, and the touching of the flag that covered the casket by the family and friends. Of course I saluted from inside the airport. Just as I have in the past for flagged draped caskets being transported via a color guard to an awaiting plane to Dover. I know so many of my letters are of a harsher tone. Mostly from frustration and concern for your and our fate in the coming months. But today I felt a little ray of hope as I watched how traveling people, strangers, stopped and watched. Just maybe you will survive this hectic, volatile period that "We the People" are experiencing. Sometimes it is the smallest of things that give us hope and change our outlook. But, I will continue to monitor the events that surround us and threaten this experiment in human freedom and this American Ideal. Hope for the best, look for the good and the positive, but forever vigilant in my assessments of the unrest that is being openly displayed in some areas of the country. Always prepared to defend family, friends, and you America. Support and defend the Constitution of the United States of America against all enemies. Foreign and domestic. And bear true faith and allegiance to the same. That is part of an Oath I swore to 46 years ago. And have swore to that Oath several times over the years. Can't and won't unswear it.

Always loyal and faithful.

    v/ r
    Dan

Dear America,

    Big tech companies are purging content on the internet. No surprise here. Censoring what is put out on the internet! They now have total/absolute control of what is being released to the public. This is what happens in totalitarian/communist countries. Should not happen in America. For example: a video of Doctors speaking of COVID 19 and how there are no cases reported of children infecting teachers. It, COVID 19, is largely passed on by the older population. There is a lot more to the video but you get my drift. But big tech companies pulled it due to political reasons masked under misinformation that could cause harm. How dare they? Talk about tyranny. It's here. Thou shall not speak against our political agenda. Not only did big tech shut down these esteemed doctors' press conferences from being seen on the internet, they shut down anyone sending the video. Double how dare they. What happened to freedom of speech in your country America? Will this letter be censored too? These political driven keepers of the worldly news might even come after me and my family. I ain't afraid of tyranny. Bring it on! Let's dance now and get it over with. My words are not just what I feel and think. There must be millions more. You need them now more than ever to speak out. Or we might just become a socialist/communist country. God help us if there were opposing views out there for people to read, hear and form their own opinion. Why, that would be blasphemy. We must only read or hear what the big tech left thinking people want us to hear. Shame on them. And shame on our elected Government Officials for allowing this to happen. The leftist person or persons responsible for censoring this video because it did not fit their view of life and self deemed it misinformation probably was not a doctor. But rather a far left goon who is controlling what they want disseminated to the public for political reasons. Damn them for violating Free Speech, Free thinking and our, We the People's, right to form our own opinions. Tyranny is upon us and cultivating. It will continue until the election in November. And if they get the power, it will most assuredly continue. Absolute Power corrupts, absolutely. Power unchecked corrupts even more absolutely. They have overstepped the boundary by miles. They have tread on every American, left or right, by suppressing Freedom of Speech. They need to be put in check. Checks and balances are built into the framework of our Great Nation. Not anymore I fear. I am outraged. I repeat, I am not afraid to face tyranny. I am not afraid to fight tyranny. My words are my weapon. Censor me. I will find a way to disseminate information. Come after me and I will fight back. This is still America, I am an American and I have Rights. I am an American and I love this country and I love you, America. Bring it on big tech. Bring it Radical Leftists. Bring it on socialists/communists. I stand ready to defend you America and our Rights as Americans. So help me God. We have much to discuss America. I will keep these letters coming.

Always faithful and loyal.

    v/r
    Dan

Dear America,

    I am an American, of the human race. Yes, not white, Hispanic, black, or other. But human. Why is it the Leftists want to categorize us as something? Count us statistically as a number. Place us into these identity boxes and watch the wedge between humans get driven so deep nothing can pull it out. I believe Liberals are just wrong on most accounts. But Leftists can be evil. Communism/Socialism is their end game. And they will not stop until America is erased and a new world order is established. Global citizen. I can assure you that I will never be, or recognize, the label of Global Citizen. Or be ruled under a marxists government. I am an American. Not a subject to be ruled by the ruling class. I will not be told I am free with no liberties. Freedom + Liberties = a true free Individual. A free American. What say you?

Always loyal, always an American.

    v/r
    Dan

Dear America,

Look America there is a lot of ordering from those in charge going on here in the Republic by elected officials due to this COVID 19. Not sure it's all Constitutionally legal. But, what do I know? No one has really challenged it. I mean Governor's and Government officials are closing down businesses. Mandating wear a mask rule. Locking down citizens. Imposing a 6 foot rule for social distancing. People are scared. Easier to control people and get them to obey. Politicians don't know what to do. They say wear a mask. We do. Where is the scientific proof that a mask even works? They don't have it yet. If they do I ain't seen it. They say stay 6 feet away from others. We do. Again, no scientific proof. They say close down your business. We do. It's only a mask. It's only a lockdown. And like good little comrades, we do. They say follow the science. Where is the science? People are scared. There is no critical thinking. No push back. We just do. Basically this is a test to see if we will follow orders from the totalitarians. Well, we have followed their orders. But, not all have. Be prepared my fellow Americans. Next, once one is available, it's only a vaccine. You must take the vaccine or you won't be allowed to go to a store, a movie, fly, or anywhere. The Government will track you. It's only a vaccine. Follow the Socialists/communists orders. We have already proven we can be herded like sheep. Believe the politicians and only the science they pick and choose. There are other viewpoints and data out there, but it ain't being shared or compared. Why? You know why. It doesn't fit the narrative. Doesn't fit in the box. Scared people will almost always do what they are told. These rules have pitted your citizens against each other. Someone sees another without a mask. And bam. They holler. Put your mask on, you're killing people. Damns't thing you could imagine. I yell back, you drive? Stop, you could kill someone. It's only a mask. It's only a lock down. It's only a vaccine. How about, it's only bullshit. Example of the politicians playing politics. Imagine if the Governor of Las Vegas, we are only imagining now, has the license to several weed dispensaries. And closes the local bars. But the casinos can open their bars. This pushes the locals to the casinos to drink and gamble. This has an adverse affect on the local bars. Hmmmm? And never closed the weed dispensaries. Hmmm again. And just for a moment imagine said Governor has ties with casinos and California and the Dems. Just might sway his thought process. Where is his heart? In his wallet and with his political ties? I'm telling you America, the political games being played here in your Republic, for the sake of power, would make you just want to slap your mule. They have no shame. Your citizens are suffering due to this power grab. And the politicians don't care. I will say it again. They don't care. It's only a mask. It's only a vaccine. It's only a lock down. It's only our Rights. It's only our Freedoms. It's only our Liberties. It should be our decisions. Wear a mask or don't. Get the vaccine or don't. Go out to a restaurant or don't. Stay home or don't. We are Free Americans. Stop the totalitarianism BS. We are not comrades. We are Americans. It's only a mask. It's only a vaccine. It's only a lock down. It's only our Freedoms!

Always faithful and loyal.

    v/r
    Dan

Dear America,

The Right to Pursue happiness. My favorite Right put to paper by our great Founding Fathers' documents. That phrase speaks volumes. Not the right to happiness, but the right to Pursue Happiness. I believe each individual must make their own bones in this life. You control your efforts to chart your course. As high as you want or as low as you want. No one should restrict others' liberties or lives. As so well put by Pete Hegseth, "this includes the government. The government is where dreams go to die." I believe Pete has captured this correctly. You, America, never intended for a large government to rule our lives and restrict our liberties. Elected Government Officials should leave elected service after a certain number of years and live the laws they create. Elected officials who spend too many years in service are suspect to being corrupted by power, greed, and are largely disassociated with the common folk. They may even be beholden to large donors and activists. This is bad juju. Why have we, as Americans, allowed this? Asleep at the wheel? Engulfed in our day to day struggles? Or, not caring? Pick one. It may be too late now to right the ship. Elected Officials are too deeply entrenched in power and control. I truly feel they do not care about the struggles of your citizens, even though they spew flowery speeches and speak words that ring hollow to my ears. How do we reinvigorate the American Dream? Re-emphasize the Right to Pursue Happiness? And recapture the Patriotism that made you great? How, without great suffering and possible internal conflict? The answers to these questions are needed soon. I fear for you America, our American Dream and the Right to Pursue Happiness without government interference.

Until next time, always loyal.

    v/r
    Dan

Dear America,

In order to form a more perfect Union, America, this Republic needs to continue to grow. Since 1776 this Experiment in human freedoms/American Ideal has made much progress. Granted it has taken much longer than expected. And we are not there yet. But that is how bureaucracies work. Slow and cumbersome. Not an excuse. Reality. We have far to go to be perfect. Let me rephrase that. Nothing is perfect, working to become more perfect to me, more perfect means the bar is high and we should always strive to become better. It will take cooperation. Resolve. And perseverance from All. And of course patience. Patience is one major ingredient missing here in America. Some have patience and some don't. So I guess the rest of the ingredients are out the window. No cooperation or compromise is achievable in today's climate. It takes everyone being dedicated to solving problems. Listening to others' ideas and finding common ground. The dedication part is the resolve portion. And the perseverance to keep dedicated to resolving the issue through cooperation and compromise. How hard is that? What is missing is the heart and the love for this Republic to make it better. You have to love America to make it better. You have to want to work together. And there are those amongst us and those elected officials who do not love this Republic. The recipe for striving to become a more perfect Union is doomed without love of country. So I ask, What are we to do? Vote out the non dedicated to make this Republic a more perfect Union? Give up? How do we undo what has been 6 decades of teaching to hate America? Perseverance. Yes. We the People, who love this country need to stand tall and persevere. Never give up, for you are never out of the fight. If we are to keep this Republic alive We the People have to find a way to calm the waters and work together. Usually that takes the leaders to set that tone. The attitude of We the People reflects leadership. It's that simple. The leaders are divisive, the People are divisive. The leaders are promoting hostility, the People are promoting hostility. Again, Attitude reflects Leadership. Let me tell you America, both sides are to blame.

Always faithful and loyal.

v/r
Dan

Dear America,

Not one mention of China during the DNC. Why is that? I heard about buy American, American this and American that. The Dems would be the first to outsource to China. Why you ask? Their rich donors? They want American citizens dependent on the government? Power? I say all of the above. If they were really for Americans they would have jumped on the Made in America, pulling our manufacturing out of China bandwagon a year ago. It was President O who said American manufacturing was not coming back. No magic wand. That came from an activist President. No concept of anything but stirring things up and a knack for flowery speeches. How pathetic. The Leader of the Free World, intelligent, but so dumb. And now we have his Ex-Vice President who wants to be President. A 47 year empty Government suit. All of a sudden has all the answers. I say hogwash. He will have many boxes to please. And many of those boxes are Anti-American with Socialist/communist ideas. A lot of people have gotten rich off setting up shop in China, a Communist Country. America is dependent on China. We must bring manufacturing and Big Pharma back to the US. We are right back to this: American or not American. Freedom with Liberties or a Government state run country. In other words a Socialists/communist country or Free America. The choice is ours. We must vote!

Always faithful and loyal.

    v/r
    Dan

Dear America,

Twenty seven words in the Second Amendment of The Bill of Rights. Gives We the People the right to bear arms. "A well regulated Militia, being necessary to the security of a free State, the right of the people to keep and bear Arms, shall not be infringed." These Powerful 27 words are and have been under attack by the Left for years. For some reason they fear your armed citizens America. Not rocket science, why? Unarmed citizens are easier to control. What's left after the weapons are gone? Rocks? Bottles? They, the Left, want people to believe that law abiding citizens should not own military style weapons. What does that even mean? All weapons could be considered military style. Any firearm is a weapon of mass destruction. Armories of our military contain all types of weapons. Even shotguns. The only weapon I can remotely think that might not be in today's military would be a revolver or lever action long gun. Of course they were at one time. So for those elected government and want to be elected government bureaucrats, who know nothing of weapons or very little, We the People see through this charade. I remind them, the right of people to keep and bear Arms, shall not be infringed. Period. Remember this, the Left wants to transform you, America. Bill of Rights, Declaration of Independence be damned in the eyes of the Radical Left. As for the Constitution, that is only something they want to change and wordsmith as part of their dream of transformation. Make no mistake America, the Left is out to change you at all cost. They will sacrifice everything and anyone that is deemed a threat to their power grab. I fear there will only be suffering and unrest in the years to come if they gain the power. Do they actually think all Americans will just surrender their weapons? I think not. Forgive them, the radical Left, for they know not what they do. The Left will try to tax, fine and confiscate each weapon and each round of ammunition. Change the laws to make it impossible for the common person to own a firearm. They will come after your We the People until they can claim victory. Remember one of the eight steps to becoming a socialist/communists country? Disarming the citizens is one of those eight steps. We the People have a small group to help us fight, the National Rifle Association. It is under attack as well. Has been for years. Not sure how long this association can fend off the government if the Left gains all the power. It may fall on the shoulders of We the People to save you, America, save our Republic, and the way of life for Americans. Support and defend the Constitution of The United States of America. Against all enemies, foreign and domestic. So help me God. I feel this will not be the only letter I write to you about this topic. Our voices must be heard in order to preserve our freedoms and liberties. There must be a common ground achieved through dialogue and compromise.

Always faithful and loyal.

    v/r
    Dan

Dear America,

The nuclear family is shrinking. Less and less two parent families. The percentage is staggeringly high. According to Wikipedia, in the 60's it was 9%. Today it is over 28% or higher according to the US Census Bureau of 2016. I believe the US leads the world in this category. Throw in the lack of quality education. Recipe for disaster. This doesn't just affect big cities. The rural areas must feel it as well. Just seems to be more prevalent in big cities. Ratio and proportion I guess. Narrowing down which cities, according to some, are the Democratic run cities. Not sure that is 100% accurate but a fair assessment given the lack of governing and resistance to allow parents to place their children in a private or charter school. Why is this? Is it their ideology? Their political views on Government? Is it the teachers union? And why hasn't this been addressed years ago? Is it because the Dems want big Government and people to be dependent on them? I think it is a little bit of both. Children need two parents. The added stability and discipline has to help. If I were a betting person, I'd bet the high percentage of single parent families and poor quality education are the major contributors to the root cause and effect of high crime and drug use in cities or rural areas. Back to my question. Why has this not been addressed and some sort of program implemented to alleviate some of this? It's no secret. Are our politicians so absorbed in keeping people dependent on Big Government that they just ignore the problem? Do they really care? Are they that ignorant and uncaring? They claim to really care. I say BS. They would rather complain and cater to all the little boxes of individual identities and grow their base one box at a time than actually solve a problem. The Government, it seems, cannot solve problems. Remember what Pete Hegseth said, the Government is where dreams go to die. Solving problems like this might just take people off government dependence and create a common bond with America. Can't have that can we. Fix the problem! I understand that fixing the single parent problem is complicated and involves an individual's decision to help fix the situation. Give people hope and the freedom to chase a Dream. Wow. Perusing an American Dream. Pursuing happiness. Actually believing in America. Why that would be sac-religious to a certain political ideology. The Dems might just lose some of their voters. Can't have that can we. Again I say BS. If you really cared about people you would fix the problem and encourage people to chase and catch their American Dream. What is so hard about loving your country? Cannot understand how hating your country that much would cause you to sacrifice the people. Humans need hope, desire, belief in living a quality life and dreams to aspire achievement. This Republic was supposed to create the common bond. This experiment in human freedoms is failing because there are those amongst us who want it to fail. Again, I say BS. Stop the hating and start being an American. Start really caring about Americans and solve problems through compromise. How hard is it? Must be really hard. All our elected officials want to do is grab the power. We the People matter. Period. Govern under the Constitution and Declaration of Independence. Stop worrying about the rich people and what they have. This is a capitalistic Republic. There will always be those who have more. Stop the BS. Fix this problem of poor quality education for all Americans children. Is that asking too much? If it is, leave office you pompous egotistical Government bureaucrats. You work for We the People and don't say you don't. That would be insulting to We the People's intelligence. To all of you elected officials who can't compromise and solve problems in the best interest of your constituents, I say on behalf of America and the ones who really care about America, Bull sh!&. Better education. Better trade schools. Create jobs. And just maybe the American Dream will come alive and restore that common bond America needs to flourish and instill the values of the nuclear family once again.

Always faithful and loyal.

    v/r
    Dan

Dear America,

Benghazi. I am usually a forgiving man. I can overlook most things and move on. No one is perfect. We all make mistakes. Lord knows I have made a bunch of them. I own up to my mistakes. But, America, I cannot find it in my heart to forgive our leaders, from the Ex-President on down for the decisions leading up to the attack on Benghazi, to the lies and deceit that followed. The cover up was a total lie to your American citizens. It was 56 days before the election and the worst situation for an incumbent President was to learn the hard way that his foreign policy in a certain region has failed. And that members of your cabinet were asleep at the wheel and sent Americans into a hotbed of trouble without any critical thinking or situational awareness. I guess they didn't see that one coming. Incompetence was abundant. And to top it off, no one, could make a decision on what to do. Things went South. People died. No American support was sent to assist those in harm's way. An Ambassador died and some others. I can only imagine the overtime the IT people put in to find that heinous video to be used as the scapegoat. Mr. Ex-President then sent one of his top butt kissers to major news channels to flood the air waves with BS. For that I can never forgive all associated with this massive CYA. I was embarrassed that America's leaders would stoop so low. How hard is it to just say." My fellow Americans I screwed up? Extreme Ownership. I would have had more respect for all involved. But no, the entire Administration acted like a third grader and covered up the massive screw up. And most of the country did not have a clue. Got away with that one Dems. Convince me otherwise and I will stand corrected. But they all know it was BS at the highest level. How long can this deceit go on? How long can a political party continue to pull the wool over the eyes of real Americans? I'm not talking about the so-called Americans who want to transform the Republic, abolish our history and retool the entire institution or those who want to instill the economic framework of Socialism to become a Communist State. I'm not talking about those who wish to become a Globalist country without borders. I am talking about Americans. Those who love this country and believe in it. We ain't changing for the lying ways of Socialists/communists. So go tell that BS to your shallow thinking radicals. But as for me, I'm gonna be the good ole American who loves this Republic and will always cherish the fruits of Freedom and Liberties. I respect straight talk. Not flowery speeches that ring hollow. I respect Extreme Ownership. Admit you screwed up, make it better and move on. So for now I'm gonna stay unforgiving to President O's administration for lying and covering up like third graders. Maybe someday I will reconsider. I salute those brave troopers who went to the rescue and held off the attack. Damn brave troopers. Real Americans. We need more like them and less of the weak kneed politicians telling us how to live our lives. God Bless them and God Bless America. Oh yeah. God, sorry I ain't forgiven those who deserted the brave people in Benghazi and then lied. Like I said. Maybe someday. What say you America?

Always faithful and loyal.

    v/r
    Dan

Dear America,

Today is another anniversary of one of your historic moments. 9/11. The day terror came to your shores and attacked your citizens. This attack left thousands dead and instilled fear in millions. America attacked. It was a shock wave that touched the very fiber of each American. You would have been proud to watch what first responders and everyday normal citizens did to help rescue the victims. Brave souls each and everyone. Then there were the passengers of Flight 93. They were actually the first group to launch a counterattack against this terrorist group. Real Americans, real heroes. What they did was stop a plane from hitting another target. The Capitol Building, where more Americans would have been killed. That flight fell into an open field where all passengers perished. I salute them and their heroic act. That day brought America together. Patriotism was high.

Citizens were openly proud of you. Your flag flew tall. We the People stood tall. We came together as a Nation. My hope is that Americans will never forget the attack, the heroes and the feeling of American Pride that swept this Republic 19 years ago. God Bless you America.

Always faithful and loyal.

> v/r
> Dan

Dear America,

In today's politically charged climate you never know what is awaiting you around a corner or on any street. Something I learned a long time ago and try to live by is this:

Escape, evade and survive. Three actions all should understand, practice and assimilate into every day living. It's how you mentally prepare for dangers and move out or not into that zone. Execute a plan to remove yourself and loved ones from that zone. Anticipate dangers, and survive. Something learned in military life or survival training. Head on a swivel. Always evaluating. Always analyzing and planning. Always surviving. Think about it for a few minutes. It's much like an athlete training until they can't get it wrong. Trained muscle reaction. Only trained mind and muscle reaction. Yes it's tiring and can wear you out mentally. I know this feeling. Lived it. Still live it to some extent. Afraid of letting your guard down in fear of getting in a bad situation without a plan. Think about entering a restaurant. Most people just walk in, sit down, hold a conversation, order, eat, pay and leave. Never think about anything else. I can't do that. You should not do that, if you want to escape, evade and survive. Enter and evaluate where to sit. Identify alternate exits. Look for places of refuge. See what can be used as a weapon. And by all means if legal, conceal carrying. Same process in a store, large crowd, movie theater or anywhere. Becomes a way of life. Escape, evade and survive. In today's volatile climate this cannot be over amplified. Start thinking. Around every corner, down every street, anywhere. Yes, America, that is where "We the People" are today. So much unrest and divisiveness. In a blink of an eye we can find ourselves in the middle of a bad situation. Just a simple drive to the local store or walk around the block can be disastrous. Have a plan. Watch and don't just look but see. Escape. Evade. And survive. America needs you. Your family needs you.

Always faithful and loyal.

    v/r
    Dan

Dear America,

I am in a defiant mood today. Think of that pot of water on the stove waiting to boil. You know, the little bubbles starting to rise to the top and getting bigger until it boils. Well, I have been on the stove on low heat for some time now. The bubbles are getting bigger. The elitists are really showing their colors. Reminds me of a book by George Orwell, "Animal Farm" I read over 45 years ago. Mr Orwell was a Democratic Socialists. There's that oxymoron again. What is Democratic about Socialism? If my memory serves me correctly the book is a lesson about Socialism/Communism written by a socialist. Mandatory reading in school. Go figure. Learning about how socialism/communism is not utopia in school. Okay. Back to the book. It's about the farm animals' rebellion against the abusive farmer. They were hoping to create a society where all animals are equal, free and happy. The pigs end up in charge after the rebellion. The self imposed leader was named Napoleon. But the rebellion is betrayed and the farm animals under the dictatorship of Napoleon end up in a state far worse than before the rebellion. The pigs become more cruel, oppressive and abusive than the humans. The animals end up exactly like the humans. Everyone is created equal, only some are created more equal. This book exposes the myth about Socialism/communism. This warning against an idealistic rebellion turning into tyranny needs to be heeded. Well by cracky, I tell you of two circumstances where it looks like there are some farm animals in our government created more equal amongst us. Instance number one. The Mayor of Chicago went to a salon to get her hair done. No problem right. Only there were ordinances that didn't allow this for the common folk. Her excuse. I am on National TV and have to look good. Pondering that. ????? Instance number two. Our illustrious Speaker of the House went to a salon in San Francisco to get her hair done. That too was a no no for common folks. I heard she said she was set up and takes no ownership of this grave violation. More of the "I am so important" BS. Well, Madam Speaker and Madam Mayor my wife, my daughters, my grandchildren and my friends are important too. Are you both created more equal? Again BS. You both are sorry excuses for leaders and are ruining American Lives with your incompetence and you don't give a damn about real

Americans. You two elected officials are the Napoleons. How about We the People just say pack your mask rule and your shutdowns. I mean by the multitudes. Millions must show their disgust. Take off the masks and shop owners open up and defy the totalitarian abuse. And don't lecture me about killing people. I ain't buying it. As Americans we should be allowed to wear or not wear a mask. Teach or not teach. Go out or not go out. We are not socialists/communists to be told how we should live our everyday lives. Leave us alone. Americans are free and should be able to decide for themselves. Keep it up Madam Speaker and Madam Mayor and you just might see Real Americans defy your BS and vote you out. Do not underestimate Real Americans. For when we come a calling, you will hear us. We won't burn cities and businesses. We won't attack people for their ideologies. We will stand for America. Freedoms and liberties. We will keep America alive. Real Americans just want the government to leave us alone and let us live our life in peace as Free People. In closing, America, I call for millions to rise up and say "No more bullshit" leftists. Peaceful, of course. We the People will remain free. Okay, little bubbles now that I have vented. Take care America and let's hope for the best. Oh yeah, vote out the pigs (Animal Farm) and vote in Real Americans who really care about America, not power and control.

Always faithful and loyal.

    v/r
    Dan

Dear America,

    I have written to you several times about compromise by our politicians and American citizens. Today's America is one roller coaster ride after another. This experiment in human freedoms is struggling. Today we, Americans, We the People, need you to continue to stand tall. Wave that torn, burnt and soiled flag so all can see it as a symbol that America is alive and there is hope that this Republic has a chance to continue to grow. That the freedoms and liberties afforded to us will always be there. Our leaders, on both sides, are failing us, We the People. Yes, it is those who govern and the biased media of this Republic that are keeping the Great Divide, as I call it, from narrowing. If they, the politicians, cannot begin to compromise, then We the People must strip them of the very power they seek. The media is another matter. It is a privilege to live in this country. Yes I said the privilege word. All American citizens have and share that privilege to live here. The root cause and effect of this great divide is power and lack of compromise with that power. Until those who govern accept that, this great Republic will continue to tear itself apart. There must be common ground. There is room to give and take, and work within the Constitution and Bill of Rights. But with all the hyperbole about transforming America, racism, and government running our lives and those who want smaller government. I don't see much common ground. All the rioting, looting and destroying property does not solve the problem. Our elected officials must be leaders and work together. One side wants the mayhem to continue. It helps their political cause in this election cycle. Some of them actually encourage it to continue. Just watch the news. Again this does not solve the problem. Only makes it worse. Both political parties will not call for or demand unity through dialogue. What a travesty. Political activists on one side and political weaklings on the other. No wonder this Republic is falling apart one piece at a time. Government will not or cannot fix it. This I have come to believe. Only We the People can fix it. One side spends energy tearing down America while telling us they want to rebuild America. President Trump's words. I actually believe that is somewhat true. And the other side, cannot make up their mind about which side to stand for. How about both sides stand for America and fix the problems together. Oh yeah, that gets in the way of power. America, you are at a tipping point and I believe that only We the People can salvage this Great Republic or destroy it. There are just not enough elected officials who believe in America as a Republic. And far too many Americans who dislike you. This idealogical difference in the Constitution and Bill of Rights needs to be closed. What say you?

Always faithful and loyal.

    v/r
    Dan

Dear America,

I am always amazed at how fate puts opportunities in front of us and our decisions from these opportunities determines our destiny. Will fate dropped an opportunity in front of me today at work. And my decision to stop and speak with a man working lead to an enjoyable learning conversation. Somehow the conversation about work transitioned to retirement and briefly brushed on politics. The man, a person I have never met, began speaking of a prophet named Kim Clement. As we parted ways this stranger recommended I google Kim Clement. Well, I did. I was mesmerized listening to his prophecies and songs. The song, The Mountain of the Lord, got my attention. The words reached deep into my soul. His prophecy in 2007 really caught my attention. He foretold that Trump shall become a trumpet for the Lord. And bring the wall of protection to this country. That Trump will go through hell for two terms. He would not be a praying President when he entered office, but would be when he left. And the economy of this country will change rapidly. Now if that doesn't make one step back and ponder for awhile. Nothing will. If you were to sit down and really study what is going on in your country America, I think you would find some interesting and notable events leading this Republic to a crossroad of fate and destiny. Of course the destiny part is predicated upon a decision. I heard something the other night during the RNC, sorry I cannot recall who said it otherwise I would give them the credit. I will try and recall the words. "When the Lord starts blessing, the devil starts messing." Ponder that and think of Mr Kim Clement's prophecy. Trump shall become a trumpet for the Lord. The Lord's blessing. Will the devil sure started a messing. Look at what is going on in this country today. The Left has spent 3 years trying to tear down our President. Mr Clements prophesy again, he shall walk through hell for two terms. I think this first term has been nothing short of hell for our President. For someone to endure the constant bashing, the nonstop negative media reports, the endless blaming of all things wrong, and the over the top smearing of his family and him. No normal person could endure without some kind of Divine intervention. Any lesser person would have packed up and left long ago. Not President Trump. He stood in there and took every punch. Sometimes I think he was hanging on the ropes just to not fall to the canvas. And after catching his breath and shaking off the brain fog he came out swinging. He just kept charging. Passing bills, pushing through Executive Orders, and fighting for the American people, your people America. He stood as tall as you have all these years. No matter what was thrown his way he kept going. Now that is true American fighting spirit. I think it starts with believing in you, America. A deep belief and love for this American Ideal and experiment in human freedoms. A belief so strong that the thought of giving up is quickly brushed aside. The Trumpet only gets louder and longer. Need I say more. I believe in this Republic. And so do others. We will stand tall. For failing you, America, is not an option.

Always faithful and loyal.

    v/r
    Dan

Dear America,

    A small ray of hope broke through the dark and gloomy words of the Democrats today. A Democrat Representative from Tennessee gave a heartfelt under your skin speech about how the BLM movement is not peaceful and will not help the cause. His story was heartfelt and genuine. Sorry I can't quote much of his speech. Basically he talked about peaceful unity and integrity and did not approve of the riots. He placed emphasis on what Dr. Martin Luther King said about not judging by the color of one's skin, but rather the character of an individual. This Democratic Representative seemed upset that all the Democrats do is focus on color. There is more to his speech but I want to stay on this color topic. I fear his speech will not resonate through his political party. Or will it get much mainstream media attention. That would go against the code and secret Main Street media handshake with the Democrats. Personally I think they will shun him because his views are not in line with the party's approach to winning an election. The Dems know that by focusing on color and beating the drums of racial hate they will keep the division alive and fuel the hate. Only one Democrat that I know of has voiced a displeasure with what is going on. The Representative I mentioned earlier. Remember, the BLM is rooted in Marxism. And recall the 8 steps to Socialism/Communism. There you have it in a nutshell. Finally a Democrat comes forward with integrity and calls what is happening by BLM and ANTIFA for what it really is. And, silence from the rest of the party. What a shame. During the entire DNC many speeches were delivered that spoke of Democracy. And these speeches were pinpointed at individuals' emotions. They even mentioned God, although the Dems had God removed from many institutions. There was so much icing smeared over their real agenda that it was appalling. It was no more than a sales pitch on steroids. There was no mention of the violence going on in some major cities. There was no mention of stripping Americans of their weapons. There was no mention of Socialized government run medical for everyone. No mention of the pact the Democratic Presidential candidate made with a Senator who is a Democratic Socialist. Now if that ain't an oxymoron. What is Democratic about a Socialist? There was little to no mention of their plan, their vision, or how they were going to pay for some of their radical agendas. There were several behind the scenes speakers but they weren't part of the big show and not widely disseminated. It was like putting lipstick on a pig and then being asked to kiss it. It's still a pig. When will all the BS stop? The Lefts Holier than Thou pompous attitude is remarkable. The perfect politicians and leaders. They can do no wrong and life will be a walk in the park under their leadership. The transformation of you, America, will be swift and darn near irreversible if pulled off. President Lincoln warned us, be careful what you teach our youth, they are the future leaders of this Republic. Boy was he right. Now what coach? All we can do now is vote for a candidate who believes in you and wants America to be great and Americans first. Fill the doom and gloom the Democrats offer with a bright future of liberties and freedom. A future as an American. A free American.

Always faithful and loyal.

    v/r
    Dan

Dear America,

In my previous letter I gave praise to Democratic Representative from Tennessee for posting his speech denouncing the violence of BLM. Well, I have heard that speech was taken down by him for fears of the backlash from the Left. Just when I thought there might be a slight chance of hope, poof, it is gone. So now I revert back to one of my earlier letters where I mentioned, the line in the sand has been drawn. There is no middle ground. There will be no compromise. You're either for America, for liberties and for freedom. Or you ain't. That doesn't mean I will give up totally on hope that there will ever be a middle ground. It only means that for now I believe there is none. Maybe the ole boy in Mississippi had it right. They are stealing a country. Real Americans are on their own to keep this American ideal, this experiment in human freedoms alive. You, America, once again will have to stand the test of time and this tidal wave of hate towards you and your flag. I am sorry. It pains me to think this is going on in this Great Republic. But you are not alone. I believe in my heart of hearts that you and I are not alone. I only hope there are many more like me who will stand beside you. Rise up and vote. Keep America, America.

Always faithful and loyal.

    v/r
    Dan

Dear America,

Ok tonight I got that ray of hope back. I heard from real Americans who love this country. Who still believe in the American ideal, this experiment in human freedom and the American Dream. Yes we have come far, but we can go further. I know we can. I once read, if you are busy rowing the boat, you're too busy to rock it. Let's all row together for a better, more just, more tolerant and a better compromising Republic. I heard from a black man, a notable politician, Mr. Tim Scott, whose family went from picking cotton to Congress in one lifetime. How great is that! Hot damn. No celebrities, no doom and gloom, no we the government will tell you how to live. Also, heard from a Cuban immigrant who cherishes you America. Supports one of my previous statements in a letter, people are building rafts to leave Socialist/ communist countries, but no American is building a raft to go to Cuba or any other Socialist/communist country. I heard of hope with substance. Not hollow words and false promises. All I heard in the DNC was what a decent man their Presidential candidate was. That America is basically evil. Hell, there are hundreds of thousands of decent persons in America. We want a leader who believes in you, America, and the American life. Our President, according to some, may not be considered a decent man, or doesn't act Presidential, but he believes in America, Americans and the American way of life. What a refreshing thing it is to hear so many want America to continue to grow and prosper. I am inspired. I heard from women, different races, all were Americans. Yes, Americans still exist. They believe in the rule of law. They believe the government should not run every aspect of our lives. That government should not be all that powerful and overreaching. That people are free. They believe that all are created equal and equal justice for all. I heard from one Republican who actually will support the Democratic nominee for President. And when asked if he supports the Democratic nominee´s statement "I will be the most Progressive President in history", that person replied, "Oh, it's just the primaries." What does that mean? That the Democratic nominee for President is lying to his base to just get votes. I said it before, and I will say it again, you cannot put the genie back in the bottle. If you are going to put people in boxes, and deploy identity politics, those in a particular box want you to support their views. Lots of boxes, lots of views. And when you don't, those in the box might get upset. Being an American is not about living in a box, it's about living outside of the box. Your identity is a Free American. Let's support America, work together to overcome the challenges of this Republic by pooling the strengths of this Republic. Row together. Grow together.

Always faithful and loyal.

    v/r
    Dan

Dear America,

All this turmoil going on now is not a 100% black white thing, in my humble opinion. It's more of an American vs a Socialist thing. The flame is being stoked by activists who use race as the fuel. And turn it into a black white thing. Their demands are rooted in Marxist's teachings. Remember the 8 steps to socialism/communism I wrote you about? I still believe all 8 are being deployed. So, what can we do as a Republic? Where will we end up in 6 months or a year from now? Keep the people divided. Create social unrest through hate and violent protests. Ensure the gap between ideologies does not close or narrow through compromise and civil dialogue. Encourage those who want to take or destroy others´ property by carefully chosen rhetoric. Make demands of dismantling the very institutions that keep a Republic civil and operating under a Democracy. Throw out fancy slogans and buzz words that drive the wedge between the citizens so deep that nothing will bring back a life of harmony or trust. Use race as a weapon whenever any conversation does not support the agenda or no intelligent retort can be made. Sell people on the fact that Whites are privileged. I am not sure I agree with " privileged " being the optimum word. Let's define the word privilege shall we. A right or liberty granted or opportunity to some and not to others. Advantages others don't have. Okay think about those words. Why is it the Democrats put everyone in a box? All white people are privileged. I say this. I sure as hell don't feel privileged just because someone wants me to say that or feel that way. I grew up in a modest home with modest means. Went to a public school and did not have lots of things others had. But I was happy to have a roof over my head, food on the table, clothes, and two pairs of shoes. If you wanted something, you worked to earn money to buy it. Some advantage that was. I spent 27 years in the military and every person there, no matter what color, religion, or ethnic background took the same tests. Wore the same clothes. Had to pass the same physical training and written tests. Had to shoot and qualify from the same distance. Disassembled and clean your weapon to the same standard. I could go on and on. I made my bones in this life. I overcame obstacles to achieve. I sacrificed years of not being with my wife and children to serve this great Republic as everyone in the military did, regardless of color. Each of us has a choice no matter of what color you are born to. Stop making excuses and go out there and overcome obstacles and go as far as you can in this life. Stop worrying about what others have. If you want a Socialists life, make a raft and paddle to Cuba or Venezuela. Here in America at least you have a choice, freedoms and liberties. So no, I will never make excuses for what I don't have. I will never want what someone else has that I cannot afford. I will never surrender my freedoms or apologize for being born white. I could have been any color and I would still be me. I earned my bones in this life and will not be put in a box to cowl before those who want me to say I am privileged. If life is tough, make an excuse to keep going. Break it down into small tasks and complete the task. There is a fire in each of us, a desire, find it and use it to overcome. Will yourself to achieve. God and only God will judge me. Not man. I am a free American. I don't see people leaving this country to go live in a Socialist/communist country. I only hear of people leaving those countries to come to America. So why in God's green earth would we, a free Republic, want to become Socialists/ communists? Makes no sense to me. Get a grip. Stop feeling sorry and go out there and make a difference in your life. It's hard and full of let downs. But keep going. Stop making excuses. Have some extreme ownership of your life, failures and successes. Be an American. Be proud of who you are and what you have. I am. Sorry, America, got on my soapbox. God Bless those who try and God help those who won't try. And God Bless you, America. Thank you for our freedoms, liberties and the privilege of living in America.

Always faithful and loyal.

    v/r
    Dan

Dear America,

Been a few days since I wrote to you, but domestic duties called for my attention. The wife and I got to spend the weekend at our property in Mississippi. Fresh air, rain, sunshine and good ole fashion hard work. There I had the pleasure of chatting with a fellow who grew up in Mississippi. His thoughts about the Transformation of you, America, the Left is speaking about, is nothing more than a group trying to steal a country. Now think about that for a second or two. Not far fetched. Kinda makes sense. Win the power. Interpret the Constitution any way they feel, ignore the Declaration of Independence and Bill of Rights and presto. A new country and the end of our Republic, you America. Probably even keep the name America, how insulting, even though you will look much different as a Socialist/communist country. That ole boy I talked to had what is referred to as a Bug Out Bag. All the essentials of surviving in the woods for extended periods of time. Meals Ready to eat. Drinking straw for filtering swamp water. Clothes. His guns and ammo. And other stuff. That tells me volumes of the state of mind of some of your Americans. People are beginning to feel that a radical change is coming. How radical no one knows. All we hear from the Left is the flowery speeches and calm delivery of them. How bad our present President is and how wonderful the Left's candidate is. They surely don't like the presiding President. What everyone is missing is this, in my humble opinion. It is not about liking the President. It's about loving or even liking America and the freedoms/liberties available. America first. Is that so bad? Oh yeah, some on the Left despise you, America. Nothing is what it seems. The Left is never wrong, no bad press. But anyone who does not agree with their agenda are evil, uncaring and racist. For the life of me I cannot understand how others do not see through the rouge. There is no mention of the violence by those who vehemently reject the Right or the current institutions. No mention of those who are creating chaos and destruction in large cities and now planning to do more of the same in the suburbs. They chant filthy words to residence and threaten to take their property because it should be theirs. Fear and intimidation. The Left does not condemn these acts. That must mean they condone it. Something really bad and violent might result if the wrong group is verbally or physically attacked. I fear this has great potential to explode. But not one peep from the Left. Again, they must condone these acts. They want it to happen? Remember the eight steps to Socialism/Communism? Right out of the play book. Mark my words, something will happen and the Left will cry party foul and claim it was a peaceful protest. Why is it they never own up to any mistakes or failed legislation or wrong doing? Are they that perfect? They sure want people to think so. Almost always, a liar, will call someone else a liar first to shift blame? The Left openly outlines a Socialist/communist agenda. How they will create jobs for all people of the United States. Why don't they say "Citizens?" Because they are not speaking of citizens. They are speaking of people who enter through open borders. That's right! Globalism. Open borders. Everyone in the United States gets free this and free that. That's all good until the country runs out of other people's money. Let me refresh your memory. What jobs did Obama/Biden create? Very little. President O, said manufacturing was not coming back. No magic wand would bring them back. Catering to China and other countries. Will the magic wand was President Trump. And they hate him for it. He made promises and kept them. Let me say again. You don't have to like the man, only love America. When will people see through the BS from the Left? Maybe too late. I say Vote, Vote and Vote out a Socialist/communist agenda. Work hard, pursue happiness and relish in freedom/liberties like no other country has. I will always pick freedom and liberties over tyranny.

Always faithful and loyal.

    v/r
    Dan

Dear America,

Either your for America or you ain't. Years ago we were taught or learned to love you. Love is unconditional. Love the good and the flaws. Over the years many have been taught not to love you and to not love being an American. There is no bond. No unconditional understanding or love of this Republic. Only how to despise the past and calls to transform our system. Color me stupid, but erasing our past doesn't change the past. Today it is cancel our 244 years of existence. Next year it will be cancel the past year. Keep cancelling everything until what? Utopia? How shallow are those who think this way? Cannot comprehend the logic or thought process. There is more in play here than that. And we both know what it is. Socialism/communism. My opinion is maybe try this: create a Pro American Party. Dissolve the Republican Party and it becomes the Patriot Party, and call the Democratic party what it really is, the Communist Party. Nothing Democratic about them these days. The Patriot party vs The Communists party. That might stop the rogue both parties are hiding behind. Again I say, your either for America or you ain't. This Republic cannot withstand the enormous internal strife that is growing from within the political parties. Something has to give. Too many We the People are not promoting the American bond. There are too many self centered, shallow thinking, narrow minded citizens of this great Republic that have no concept of Patriotism. How is that? I default to our education system. That will be another letter totally devoted to The Teachers Union and their self serving ways. But for now there is more to deal with. One crisis at a time. Yes, America, I am rambling. If this Republic doesn't get the political party situation in line with real Americans issues the Republic will collapse. Won't happen this election cycle but something to build on. So how do we overcome the 60 plus years of educating our youth to hate you America? How do we overcome the political divide? And how do we overcome the media bias that spews more false narratives than truths? Vote! Americans must vote to Keep America, America. That's how. Stand up to the BS. Say enough is enough. Teach people and reinforce how great the Republic can be with all the freedoms and liberties afforded us by our founding Fathers. Keep this experiment alive in human freedoms/ liberties. Keep America Great and Alive.

Always faithful and loyal.

    v/r
Dan

Dear America,

Today I had the privilege of hearing a great story about a real Patriot, an American. The story was about a 100 year old American, and a Navy Veteran. He was stationed on a ship in Pearl Harbor when the Japanese attacked. His job was to climb to the crow's nest, approximately 75-90 feet above the deck and be a look out. Japanese planes were flying all around, large Navy guns were throwing artillery and utter chaos was going on all around him as he perched high in the air performing his duty. Takes bravery to act out what you are trained to do in combat. After surviving that attack he was on a ship towards the end of the war approximately 250 miles from Guam. And once again attacked. That ship was hit by a torpedo. The young sailor survived that and the ship sailed 250 miles to Guam at 2 miles an hour. During the time it took for the ship to get to Guam the Japanese signed the treaty ending the war with Japan. Of course he and his wife of 57 years went on to live a wonderful wife, raise 4 children and enjoy 13 grandchildren. The Navy veteran did not stop his service to you America after he left the Navy. He volunteered to help other veterans. And still might be volunteering for all I know. This true American has a great love of this Republic. I heard him say during a short interview that he would help people, who do not love this country, to pack up and leave to another country of their choice. He said there is no greater country in the world than America. I would like to meet him, shake his hand and tell him what a Great American I think he is. I would also like to know more about him, but I think I know how he feels. There is a feeling I get every time I see a flag or write to you. That is how he must feel. God Bless him, his wife, their children and their grandchildren. And I thank him for his service and volunteer work. Now ain't that just a real good feel good story?

Always faithful and loyal.

   v/r
   Dan

Dear America,

Americanism! We The People in order to form a more perfect Union......Americans should be united by a common belief in The American Ideal. You, the Red, White and Blue. A unique way of life where all people are created equal and share the same liberties and freedoms. So far in the 244 years of your existence We The People have made, in my opinion great strides towards the created equal part. Are we there yet? No! We can be with the right leadership, the right education, continued perseverance and the restoration of Patriotism. There are those amongst us who wish to grow government, orchestrate the decline of you, and control us, We The People. We are Americans. I will not apologize for being an American or surrender that belief in you. If our two major political parties cannot or will not defend Americanism, then by God, We The People must create a new party. It is time to unite all Americans and achieve a higher respect and acceptance of all citizens. It is time to take back our education system and teach the true history. The good and the bad. Learn from it so the bad is not repeated. Restore a new and improved policing of the citizens. One that serves and protects with dignity and keeps law and order in the forefront. We The People should acknowledge the fact that we have gotten better and need to continue to improve as a Nation, One America. Unite us America. Ring loud and true. Display the Red, White and Blue and maybe, just maybe enough true Americans will hear your bell toll and answer the call.

As always, faithful and loyal.

v/r
Dan

Dear America,

The Dems will not or are unable to articulate an intelligent rebuttal or debate over political differences. I'm willing to compromise. Why aren't they? The conversations usually end in someone being called a racist, the main default, or other derogatory names. Or, I don't like Trump. How shallow. It's no wonder as most higher educational institutions will not tolerate other political viewpoints such as Conservative ideas to be expressed. I thought the Dems were the party of tolerance. Protestors are allowed to interrupt speeches that are contrary to what they believe. Why is that? Places of higher education are supposed to be where one goes to expand one's knowledge and broaden their views of the world. Become more worldly. Digest information, research, read, share ideas and form intelligent well informed opinions. It is not just the higher places of education where certain histories and ideas are suppressed. It starts in the lower tiers of education. True American history is not taught today in many schools. There are even schools who are planning on teaching Project 1619. Our youth are taught that America was founded on racism and built on hate. It appears that the brainwashing begins early on. For the life of me I cannot understand how there are those who hate you, America, that much, yet they remain here. They want transformation of this country and a remake of the systems framed by our Founders. Create a utopia of Government run everything. Do they think that all the freedoms and liberties they enjoy today will remain? Maybe they don't realize that the freedoms and liberties printed in our framework will diminish. Maybe they don't care. What do they think will happen? No critical thinking on their part. Remember the 60's and early 70's? There was a chant that went something like this " If you don't like America, then leave it". Look where we are today. I would like to offer this to all those educated idiots and haters. I will personally buy 2 tickets for 2 haters of you, America, a one way ticket to Siberia, Venezuela or the former Yugoslavia. Let's see how they fare there. Hell, I up the two tickets to five. Goodbye America haters. If our education system continues this course of non teaching American history, accentuating the American evil, and not fixing the education system for all to learn, you will cease to exist. It's past time for American's to take a stand. Vote. Vote. Vote.

Vote away the socialist/communist movement. Do not accept the hate and demands of a few radicals. Let's keep our freedoms and liberties, reject the transformation and continue to build a better America. An America that is a shining symbol of freedom, liberty and justice for all.

Always faithful and loyal.

    v/r
    Dan

Dear America,

What a country we live in. So much drama. So much divisiveness. So much controversy. So much unknown and indecisive direction from our elective officials. They are afraid. They are frozen by political insecurities. And the pursuit of power. They have become totalitarian in one breath and forgiving in another. Dependent on what political agenda is being played. For example, due to the COVID-19 endemic they project a military style leadership, do as I say or else. But if there is a protest/riot that benefits their cause, they turn a blind eye. Cannot attend Church. Cannot go to school. Cannot go to restaurants. Cannot go to work. Must remain at a prescribed social distance. Must wear a face covering. And so on. Thou shall not do this or that. So saith the Governors, so saith our elected officials. What about The Bill of Rights, Amendment I. The right of the people to peacefully assemble. Isn't going to Church a peaceful assembly? A family going to a funeral is a peaceful assembly. A family eating at a restaurant is for most, a peaceful assembly. I guess not. But for thousands to protest/riot/loot/destroy property equals peaceful assembly that negates the Governor's orders. How absurd is that. And what about Amendment I, the Congress shall make no law respecting an establishment of religion, or prohibiting the free exercise thereof. But a Governor can restrict. Since when is the Governor the Congress? The Congress cannot restrict our freedoms/ liberties, but a State Governor can. I don't get it. Must be a state vs federal thing. I guess We the People cannot make the righteous choice to protect ourselves. We must need the government to tell us. I understand that the Declaration of Independence states that to secure our rights, the Governments are instituted among men, deriving their just powers from the consent of the governed, that whenever any form of Government becomes destructive to these ends, it is the Right of the People to alter or abolish it, and institute new Government. There is more to it but my question is, By what authority do Governors and elected officials have on ordering a complete shutdown/lockdown of its citizens over a virus? I fear there is a partial political agenda lurking behind these decisions. Hard to prove but worthy of speculation. It goes unchallenged and is reinforced by the media. Propaganda 101. What say you America?

Always faithful and loyal.

   v/r
  Dan

Dear America,

Okay. I am going to ramble so keep up. You ain't that old. Maybe a little beat down and war fatigued. Nothing new to you. Hell, we're all a little frazzled these days. Here we go.

Critical thinking in decision making and extreme ownership of one's actions are not the phrase of the day recently. Most don't know what that means. They think that if they are morally correct, facts be damned.

The Dems plan to reap the benefits from the chaos they have created and continue to exploit. They are counting on a victory and total transformation this time. The kraken is released in their minds. And it's running rampant.

BLM is not what people think. Most have never read or questioned their Mission Statement. Is ending capitalism their end goal?

Destruction of the country for what. Power and money. They speak of equality and leveling the playing field. But not for the elite. Everyone else will live a struggled life. And feel the real burn of Socialism.

In my opinion, the Democrats do not realize that their hatred of the Republicans/Conservatives is obvious. Do they actually think we never studied history? Not one Democrat voted to abolish slavery. A Republican President led that charge to abolish slavery and perserve the union. It appears, the Democrats continue their hate and blame everyone else of racism. The elected officials of both parties have done very little to assist blacks with the opportunity to acquire a quality education and live the American Dream. Where are their plans to improve education for the inner city or impoverished people of all races spread across your vast land mass?

Open debate by Dems. Never. We are supposed to be an open society, but Dems want a closed society and sensor ideas that do not align with their ideologies. Cancel culture has repercussions. What are they afraid of? Exposure through open conversation that exposes them. Honest debate. How selfish and narcissistic.

Now they attack God. Christianity. Is their hatred rooted in authority? Loss of power? Loss of control? One man? It's not about confederate statue demolition. They are erasing their own history. They are attempting to create a utopia that can never, as proved throughout history, succeed. What dark force is this. This is a movement to abolish capitalism and destroy our governing institutions. In God We Trust, may be one of the more important stressors. Something greater than police abuse has sparked all of this. There is much to worry over. It is becoming a dark Republic. One so complex, volatile, divisive, and without critical consideration for the extended outcome. I see nothing good long term from this power grab. But if it comes to their victory and implementation of these radical ideas, then, you, America may cease to exist. And the "We the People" will get what we deserve, unless we rise up and stop it now. Fear not America. You will always live in my heart. The struggle for you will never be over. I am never out of the fight. Even in death. Someone will carry the flag. I do believe this. Or there is no hope. Without hope and faith, we fail. We fail, you fail America.

Always faithful and loyal.

> v/ r
> Dan

Dear America,

Your Americans are continuing to struggle under the current events that have plagued them recently and the Republic is spiraling out of control. Americans are scared. Scared of the COVID. Scared of economic shortfalls. Scared of the rising violence. Scared to send children to school. Scared of going to work, even if they have work. Scared of not having work. Scared from lack of hope. Scared of being a particular race. Scared no one will come and save them. Scared of dying. Scared to the point of irrational thinking. Just plain scared. And the unfortunate conclusion a lot of scared Americans are drawing is, the Government must save them. The Government does not save Americans. Dreams and salvation requests that go to the Government wither on the vine and die. The elite of the Government like to think they can save Americans, but politics, power and egos get in the way.

Americans need to save themselves. It was true Americans who built this Republic. It will be true Americans who save it. Americans used to be strong and worked through tough times. But many years of educators weakening our youth through Socialists teachings have built a population of dependency and softened self preservation. And created a culture of expecting Big Government to tell them how to live their lives. What happened to regular Americans, doing regular things, to overcome irregular setbacks in life? Have we become so soft, so dependent, so selfish, and so self centered that we need the Government to hold our hand, rub our head, tell us happy things and give us a safe space to go to. Where are the leaders in America? Where are the words to unite us? I fear there are no leaders stepping forward to lead the charge. I fear there are no words coming soon. Who will rise above all this divisiveness, all the evil rhetoric, all the doubt, and lead, We the People, back to Freedom, Liberty, and the continuation of this great experiment in human freedoms? We await that leader to step forward and lead us back to you America, the American Dream and the American freedoms. God Bless the Human Race and the American way of life. Let the experiment continue.

Always faithful and loyal.

v/r
Dan

Dear America,

Today I was going to write to you about something else. But I am compelled to write to you about the Right to Defend ourselves. The American world has gone mad. A couple in Missouri is under attack by government officials for trying to defend themselves. A basic fundamental right. The Second Amendment. This poor couple were trying to fend off what they perceived as a threat to themselves and their property after a mob broke down a gate to enter the community. They felt threatened and could not, as reported, get police to respond. That is how the story is told as far as I can understand. Their only crime appears, from what I understand is: being armed, owning property, being unafraid to defend themselves, being lawful in exercising their rights, and standing up to the mob mentality of intimidating others. Now they are being charged with some very weird criminal charges. In my opinion, they appeared to lack training in when to deploy their weapons when confronted in a hostile situation. Brandishing a weapon is not a good idea. I even heard they were guilty of owning property at the expense of indigenous people. Not my words. Words of TV talk show people who go unchecked and spew pure BS. How absurd is that. Our history haunts us again. Hard to comprehend. What the hell does today's actions have to do with the actions of 244 plus years ago? Way out of control thought process. No one should ask for retribution for not having what people have now and for what they don't have due to what someone else did over 244 years ago. Figure that one out. Makes my head spin. I say pull your adult pants up, get smart, make your own bones in this life, work hard to get your own stuff, stop wanting government to give you stuff, stop living in the past, lobby smartly to enrich the future, quit worrying about what others have, stop looking at each individual as a specific race but rather as a member of the human race, stop intimidating others and expect them to just roll over, stop the politics that make normal Americans lives frustrating, stop the insanity of thinking utopia is Socialism/Communism. We the People have a right to defend ourselves or the right of people to keep and bear arms, shall not be infringed. When will all this insanity stop? Can't we just live our lives as Americans, enjoy life liberty and freedom? I guess some people cannot. They are just so miserable and ungrateful for living in America. I ask you America, can you send those ungrateful people an eviction notice? I fully support the Second Amendment and will forever defend it. God Bless, you, America.

Always faithful and loyal.

    v/r
    Dan

Dear America,

    This weekend I had the pleasure of being on the Gulf Coast in Mississippi. Spent some time at the house in the woods and enjoyed the fresh air, sunshine, open spaces and family time. During this visit two of my granddaughters and I went to the coast highway to shop at a souvenir store. To my surprise I came across several hundred jeeps and large crowds. It was a Jeep-n-the-Coast event. Several American and Trump flags were being flown and people, Americans, were actually just hanging out exercising their liberties. In many states this would have drawn sharp criticism and possibly fines and/or arrest. Why? You ask. COVID, and the social distancing/wear a mask thing. But not at the gathering on the coast we drove by. There are those who would be yelling as loud as they could about irresponsible people spreading the virus that could kill others. Really! And who are these people who fear the virus to the extent of sacrificing civil liberties and jobs only to hide from the inevitable. Yes, by keeping our distance, wearing a mask and being cautious the virus may not spread as fast. But it will spread. It is the most vulnerable that should consider exercising caution, if they so desire. And, the ones who fear it to the extent of social isolation. Let them exercise their rights to do just that. If people want to gather, they know the risks, then let their conscience be their guide. The country is torn over this virus. Economic challenges are knocking at the door. Some in our government are all in on isolation and total control. I think some genuinely care. But I also think many are exploiting the situation for political reasons. This is an election year and many want the power to implement their form of government. They use the very institutions they despise to destroy the institutions. What a travesty. Some want a vaccine for the virus before reopening businesses and schools. I have my doubts about a miracle drug any time soon. I hope one is discovered. But there are viruses that exist without a vaccine. If a certain political party wanted to ruin the economy, have control over the people, and restrict liberties, this is the time. The virus has afforded those in power to push a certain agenda toward the transformation of you, America. Are the people resisting this control over their liberties being irresponsible? Or are they just saying enough is enough? Rebels with a cause. After all wasn't it rebels who founded this country? You know, the colonials. They gave the double six shooter banger salute to the King. Maybe that's what, We the People, are doing now to those who wish to transform us. Speaking of the virus. How is it that the virus seems to have appeared in Wuhan China first? Coincidence? There is a lab that works with bio stuff there. And at a time when our, America First Prez, has imposed sanctions on China that have been effective. And this virus, from what I hear, is a strange little booger. I have to ask. If the virus came from bats, how did the bats get it and transmit it to humans. And if from bats, why not some remote cave in a jungle or rainforest? Very strange to me. Wuhan???? If someone wanted to cripple an economy, impose suffering without regard to human life or strife and gain control, then nothing like a virus to wipe out a few million people. Just my spidey senses tingling. Connecting the dots is difficult and bears some looking into and concentrated pondering. We may never know the real story. Maybe it did come from bats. Only the final outcome is yet to be seen. But this coincidence and sequence of events sure plays into the Globalism fanatics, power grabbing political players across the world and the desire of economic dominance of some. What do I know? I am just an American who wishes only to be left alone. I obey the laws, pay my taxes and work hard in the pursuit of happiness. I want, small government (part of being left alone), to enjoy freedom with liberties, and to keep you, America, alive.

Always loyal and faithful.

    v/r
    Dan

Dear America

    Cancel culture is amongst us. What that is exactly I am not sure. But it sounds like tyranny to me. Totalitarian type of government rule. No debate. Just cancel something someone feels is offensive. Your founders wanted to create a more perfect Union. Will that takes time, we must grow and evolve as a Republic. There is no debate that in the 1700's the world was different. Over 200 years have passed and You have changed. Americans have changed. Civil discussions must take place and incorporate this change. Erasing history is not possible. You just can't take it back. People will still remember. Evolve. Learn. Move forward and not repeat past sins. All countries have a past. Good and bad. Why is it so hard for Americans to move forward and at least recognize some progress has been made. Always room for improvement. But dialogue is required by civil adults willing to sit down and discuss, compromise, and respect other viewpoints. America, I ask you, why is it so hard for your highly paid and pampered elected officials to do this? I believe it is power. One side wants total control over our lives and the other is weak and unsure. You need strong sensible leaders to lead us. It is We the People who will ultimately decide. My fear is so many of, We the People, are misinformed, misguided, and just plain ignorant of how great you, America, can be. I can't predict where all this is going but my gut tells me You are in trouble and nothing good will become of this situation we are in unless enough of, We the People, stand up against this tyranny. Where are the voices of American's? I hear nothing but TV reporters spewing BS. No real leader has stepped up to control this and take charge. I stand corrected. One has, but he is much hated and has little backing from his political party. His party cowers to keep their status as elected officials. Many books have been written exposing all the tyranny and underhanded tom foolery going on. But, no one with power or the gall has risen to organize against the Socialist/Communist movement because it is now cloaked in racism and our past sins. You are in a conundrum. We the People are in a conundrum. Wish I could be more cheery and speak of less glum but this Republic is in chaos and snowflakes seem to be in charge because the elected officials want them to keep You in disarray. It serves their cause. There are elected officials who say "If you believe you are morally right then you don't have to be factually correct". (Or words to that effect). What does that even mean in real life? We are governed by morons. Some want to dismantle not just the police but You, America. They go unchallenged. America we need your help if we are to keep the American Ideal alive, live free and enjoy the liberties of that freedom.

Forever loyal, faithful, and optimistic.

   v/r
   Dan

Dear America,

The complete transformation of America is taking place. And we sit by and do nothing. There is a strategy here. There is a tier of elite and a tier of anarchists that seek to carry this transformation to its completion. Erase history. Suppress speech. Disarm the populace. Take over the Government. Look at Venezuela. And earlier governments that have fallen. There is a script, a plan, and it is funded and organized. When will Americans organize and stop this movement? Who will lead us? Too many do not want to believe. And when they do, it will be too late. May already be too late. Too many will do nothing. The Democrats say nothing. Presidential candidate says nothing. Violence through silence. We will wake up one morning and everything will be different. And most will be surprised. Don't be. Initiate critical thinking. Don't put your head in the sand. Don't just look. But see. It's not okay to say this will pass, it will be okay and everything will be normal. Your spider senses should be tingling. If not, you are living in a bubble of denial. Give it some thought. Over 50 years of Socialist hate America has been taught in our education system. Connect the dots. Be ready. If it happens, we were warned. If it doesn't, then rejoice. Do nothing then suffer the results. We should not accept or recognize the transformation of our Country quietly, let your voice be heard. Inertia, a force will continue until met by an equal or greater force to change its course. Life, liberty, and freedom just might be that greater force. What say you?

Always faithful and loyal.

    v/r
    Dan

Dear America,

I know I am only one voice among 330 million plus or minus. That makes it pretty hard to be heard. My one vote is heard. But my voice is not. My view points are not. Am I irrelevant? I am only heard through writing our elected officials way up on the food chain. By the time my voice reaches them, if it does, it has to be so distorted that it is nothing like what I have said or meant. How messed up is that? Why bother you ask? The same reason you continue to fly that worn and tattered flag. Because I believe like You believe. We the People believe. That is why I write to you. You're a good listener. I would love to spend just one hour with the Democratic nominee for President. Yes, the one with 47 years of Government experience. And one hour with the present President, the one with 47 months. How awesome would that be? Here is what I would ask and/or say.

To the Democrats nominee:
1. Would you favor improving on O' Bama care to make it better and not be a 100% Government run medical plan? We the People do not want big Government. Controlling health care is like controlling over 50% of the economy. No bueno. Would you compromise?
2. Would you leave the Second Amendment intact? You know those 27 words. Stop going after the weapons. Go after the criminals with weapons. Could you do that?
3. Will you tell the Socialists/communists of your party to stop pushing to dismantle capitalism? And would you denounce Socialism/communism in America?
4. Would you bring our jobs back from China? After all they are a Communists country. Could you do that? Can you commit to America first and prove it?
5. How would you stop the violent destructive protest ruining businesses and people's lives?
6. Will you control the flow of illegal immigration at our borders?
7. Will you push for term limits for our elected officials? Career politicians appear to have too much power and

seem to not act in the best interest of We the People. Let them serve, leave and live the laws they implement.

8. Will you swear not to raise taxes on the lower and middle income citizens, and not regulate and tax small businesses out of business?
9. Will you not Force the radical Green New Green deal down Americans throats?
10. Will you renew the permits to allow fracking to continue? I'm not asking about banning. But renewing permits. It is a yes or no answer.
11. Those 10 questions would tell the tale of the Democrats, and their agenda. I doubt if he could answer any of them honestly. Oh yeah, I would require straight talk, not the Potomac two step. No bullshit answers..

To the present President I would ask the following 7 questions and say.

1. How would you improve on O'Bama care and keep the best parts of it and allow choice for private health insurance? Choice matters to Americans. No complete Government run healthcare. Oh yeah, and keep pre-existing conditions for those who need it?
2. Will you continue to keep America a sovereign nation and control Immigration?
3. Will you continue to pressure China and keep bringing out jobs back to America? This is important.
4. Will you cut taxes again for the lower income citizens and create more jobs that help those who really need to live the American Dream. How?
5. Will you continue to denounce Socialism/ communism in America.
6. What will you do to create an atmosphere of cooperation and compromise between all elected parties? What can you do differently if re-elected to ease the divisive atmosphere. Attitude reflects leadership.

7. Will you push for term limits. Career politicians appear to have too much power. They need to serve, leave and live by the laws they create.

Same thing to the present President no BS answers.

Wouldn't that be a hoot. Of course that will never happen. Hells bells, the Debate Moderators can't ask these questions. Make me wonder why. But it is something to ponder about. I guess we will see what the genius moderator will ask at the first debate coming soon to our TV. It ought to be quite a show. I will write to you after the debate.

Always faithful and loyal.

    v/r
    Dan

Dear America,

So, last night was the first debate between the Present President and the Democratic Nominee. As expected it was heated and divisive. Much like our country. Unlike any debate I have witnessed in my lifetime. I feel the questions were not centered more on policies and how to achieve them. Some appeared to be personal and not well thought out. Seemed a tad lopsided. My previous letter I had some questions that I thought would be answered with substance and show vision into how each would lead/guide the Republic. But, no. One was so personal it dwelled into the taxes of the incumbent President. Why? Big deal if he paid so little as a wealthy person. He only followed the tax codes established by our elected officials. Okay, back to the debate. At times, most of the time it was out of control. Interruptions and bickering. Most probably missed this but it was the Democratic Nominee who interrupted first. Three times actually. Watch it and see if I am wrong. I will stand corrected if proven wrong. The President did, in my opinion, interrupted way too much. Should have let the other guy speak more. I personally believe a leader should listen more. But, take the incumbent for example. He has been under 24/7 bashing from the media since before he was elected. How about an attempted coup/impeachment. I believe there has been sufficient evidence exposed that may very well support this. The previous administration not only knew about it but allowed it to grow. So I don't really blame the President for being a little over the top at the debate. It was really hard to follow and understand what was being said. Bottom line, very little substance from either of the candidates. Terrible questions, in my humble opinion by the moderator. And each candidate was trying to outdo the other. A couple of things I took away from the debate was this:

- Democratic nominee blames the President for over 200,000 COVID deaths in this Republic. How absurd is that. The President didn't release the COVID. He tried to curtail it. I feel he did the best he could. How dare the Left blame someone for something they could not have done better.

- The Moderator asked one to condemn White Supremacy. I found this weird. Because the one asking has condemned it multiple times since 2016. Plenty of videos supporting that.

That's about it. I surely hope the next debate is better.

Or better yet, no more debates. Let them run around and just hold rallies and town halls. The debates and the moderators questions are so calculated anyway. What say you America?

Always faithful and loyal.

v/r
Dan

Dear America,

    Quick letter tonight Ole Friend.

    From the bottom of my heart America, I Thank you for our Freedoms. Long may they live. I sure hope that people remember this country was founded by rebels that wanted to be free. The colonials overcame the tyranny of a King to establish and build a Nation. Let us hope We the People can overcome our differences and maintain this Great Republic of Freedoms and Liberties. God Bless you, America.

Always faithful and loyal.

    v/ r
    Dan

Dear America,

Tonight on my commute home from work this odd thought crept into my brain busing group. Joe Biden will become America's COVID President. So many Americans are afraid of COVID that they feel he is the protector and cure all. COVID IS A GIFT TO THE LEFT. Economic recovery be damned. Stop COVID! How shallow thinking can Americans be. And to top it off. Vice President elect Harris would be in the shadows molding policy that mirrors the San Francisco radical ideologies. Scary I know. I wonder how Americans feel about living like the San Francisco folks. Let there be no mistake. The transformation of America will take place under the Biden/Harris administration. I shuddered as this thought process ran through me. And the reality that the America I have known and loved, this experiment in human freedoms and American ideals could dissolve. That my Ole Friend scares the hell out of me. I hope that people see through all the word salad of the politicians and vote for America. I for one am tired of the BS from both sides. Vote for America. The Land of the Free and the Brave. Vote out the transformation of America. Or live with the consequences. I hope that thought of Biden/Harris winning never crosses my my again. God help us Americans. And God Bless you, America.

Always faithful and loyal.

    v/ r
    Dan

Dear America,

I know some of my letters are long and I get on the soap box and carry on. But these are trying times. Our American way of life is on the fringes of changing forever. And it troubles me. I believe in you and this Republic and want it to grow and carry on. That being said. This letter will be short.

COVID 19.

I have written you before about this but just want to share some thoughts with you

It's okay to be afraid. It's okay not to be afraid. But respect it for what it is. A dangerous virus. It should not control our lives. But it is. Maintain good hygiene by washing your hands, use hand sanitizer, wipe areas down and keep some distance between you and others. This virus may not go away any time soon. A vaccine may not be made that fully controls it. It's okay to be afraid. It's okay to not be afraid. Respect it and do what your heart and mind tells you to do. Be wary of the Government telling you what to do. Listen and then decide. Live your life as a free American. I am not sold that lockdowns are the cure all. It seems the Government gets fixated on one thing and doesn't pull the string to see what the other repercussions are. Self perform critical thinking and execute. It's okay to be afraid. It's okay to not be afraid. Respect the virus. Listen and make your own choice. But respect other Americans' choices. We really don't know the truth. It's okay to be afraid. It's okay to not be afraid. Respect it. Respect others. Just wanted to share that with you my ole friend.

Always faithful and loyal.

    v/r
    Dan

Dear America,

Okay. Took a few days off and went South. Had grass to cut, weed wackin to do and tractors that needed attention. Just imagine for a minute, if the Radical Left takes over, fossil fuel will be extinct but our 10 1/2 acres of grass, trees and wet lands won't be. Gonna be some big batteries to run those mowers. And lots of them. By the way, where will all the old batteries be stored? Oh yeah, those batteries still have to be manufactured from raw materials. Hate to even think about it. I bet those ever greener's don't think about country folks and farmers when they yell save the planet/climate change/new green deal. I see nothing in our crazy world has changed in the last 5 days. Just as crazy and just as divided. While I am on the subject of climate might as well throw out my 2 cents on that topic. This will drive the tree huggers and new green deal people nuts. So what! Past the point of trying to reason for now. Two sides to every coin, you fanatics. Save the Earth. Oh boy that's deep. The world will end in 10-12 years they chant. Even deeper thinking. We are all doomed if the Republic doesn't rejoin the Paris Climate Change thingy. Give it a rest. Several points I want to express here so keep up Ole Friend.

1. The earth will eventually destroy itself, high probability of that. It's a planet! Maybe in 1 year or a billion. Who knows.
2. The sun will eventually give out and most likely take earth with it. Stop that one radicals
3. Let's call this climate change/new green deal what it really is. Another way for Big Government to control our lives. And a big portion of the economy.
4. Yes, I agree we can continue to clean up the waters and air. News flash. Been doing that since the 70's I think. And yes we can do better and continue to improve the process, thank you Dr. Deming.
5. Americans can not do it alone. All countries have to commit to at least the rudiment environmental clean up stuff.
6. Let us not get too crazy about this New Green Deal. I mean jump off the deep end cause the world is going to end in 10-12 years. Breathe radicals and relax. If that was

true might as well party for the next few years and let it happen cause there ain't time to reverse it. Back to reality. Implement some strategies and improve on them. We the People do not want the Government overreaching. We will be taxed into poverty and forced to drastically alter our lives at our expense while Big Government stuffs radical changes down our throats. Remember Dr. Deming, continue to improve the process. Listen to the science, only both sides, for a change. Have open civil debates compromise.

Okay, said enough. The lefties will have a field day with those statements. Sorry I don't fit in your box radicals. My bad.

Middle road here. Compromise. Keep improving on cleaning the environment and let us live our lives. I wonder what would happen if several scientists sat in a room, equal numbers representing both sides of the coin, and had a dialogue. I personally think one side is cherry picked to just support one philosophy. Don't hear much from those who think otherwise. And is there really enough evidence to support some of the stuff being tossed out there? I don't know. Need lots more info from both sides. Yes, I believe that over 7 billion people do have an impact on the earth and climate. But is it really that catastrophic? Do humans really control the number of hurricanes? And are all the wildfires contributed to climate change? I say no. Most fires are a result of some bonehead being really dumb or intentionally starting a fire. Not to mention that lack of forest management that just might contribute to the fire going out of control. Don't hear much about that do we. Well kept secret. Wouldn't want the other side of the coin exposed. Someone might engage in critical thinking and have a different opinion. Can't have that can we. If the Dems want your opinion, they will give it to you. I guess it is just easier to blame climate change. Do I believe the earth goes through warming and cooling cycles? I do. Remember, America, I am a simple man. Do I believe a meteor or massive volcano eruption can have long lasting effects on climate? Yes. Just ask the dinosaurs. They surely didn't impact climate change with fossil fuels. Sorry, sometimes I get carried away. That's what free thinking, having the liberty to self express and exercising my

Freedom of Speech does to me. And I have you, America, to thank for those freedoms. God Bless America and the rest of the planet. And, God Bless the sun and planet Earth.

Always faithful and loyal.

>   v/r
>   Dan

Dear America,

Everyday I want to write to you about how great this country is. About great events that have taken place. Lately, any great event is quickly over shadowed by tragedy or wicked doings. Or just plain outrages behavior. The madness just won't stop. For a brief moment today I had the pleasure of speaking to a young black man, who is a devout Christian, a hard working man whom I have spoken with on a few occasions. We chat about religion, politics, the world in general and family. What a great American man living the American Dream. I found out today he is about to have his seventh child. You should have seen his face light up when he told me. A Proud Papa. I know he is a man of integrity and faith. He never complains. Always happy and positive. His faith is deep and he will not be moved on his beliefs. That is how We the People, who love the Republic feel. We should not be moved because there are those amongst us who do not believe in you. This is our country. Not a country for the non believers to change or steal. They are so misguided. At center stage is racism. A very difficult topic to discuss. The non-believers are focused on one issue. Systemic racism. Almost every issue is about racism. And almost every dialogue that goes against the non believers point of view is labeled racism. I do not believe a society can focus on just one issue and survive. It will consume that society. Some schools are even thinking of teaching our youth from the book Project 1619. That's not teaching. It is indoctrinating. In my humble opinion. Teach all viewpoints, good and bad. No critical thinking appears to be in play. Indoctrination of this alone could pit children against parents. Have devastating effects on the young. Could they not begin to despise their parents for being a particular race? Could the youth begin to despise themselves? I hope this is thought through with intelligent dialogue before it is implemented. I ask you, America, how can a country be labeled systemic racist if said country elected a Blackman as President twice? How is that possible? I do not believe racism is systemic in our Republic. I believe it is over emphasized and politicized to win an election and cause disruption in our society. I believe there are those who have embellished the idea of systemic racism. I further believe that the inequality movement has been hijacked by those who want to dismantle Capitalism. Racism will never be totally erased from this earth. It is present. Good should over shadow it. Some form of prejudice or racism will exist as long as humans walk this earth. Utopia does not exist. At least I have not seen it. Living in harmony can exist in a Republic United. All we can do is accept it exists, teach our children to accept others and respect others no matter their color, religion, gender or sexual orientation. We should not accept any form of racism or discrimination displayed. Condemn it and continue to improve as a Republic. Seek a balance in how it is taught and delivered. Educate. Yes we need police reform, justice reform and equality for all. United we stand. Divided we fall. This Republic could very well be on a course to fall if We the People don't wake up and start believing and stop hating. Fix the problems through dialogue and compromise, not violence.

Always faithful and loyal.

>   v/r
>   Dan

Dear America,

This is a text I received from one of my daughters last night. I have to share it with you.

"I forgot to tell you! Last night while shopping I saw an elderly man in one of the motorized carts with a marine veteran hat. I walked away and felt the need to turn back towards him. I noticed he was fumbling with something. He was having a difficult time because his hands were shaking quite a bit. As I walked towards him to ask if he needed help, he was able to untangle his mask. He proudly put on a mask with the American flag on it. I walked up to him and I said thank you for your service. I had to say it again because he did not hear me at all. I raised my voice a little louder and he smiled and responded with a thank you. I also said, "God Bless America." I immediately looked around to see if anyone heard me. Why did I feel a tinge of fear for stating something I feel and believe? From that moment on, I decided I do not need to feel the need to be silent about being proud of the United States of America. As I walked away from a man who would have died for this country, tears welled up in my eyes because I am saddened that other people do not feel the way I feel of the US of A. What can WE do to ensure that every single American feels and knows the opportunities, not oppression, they have in the greatest Republic this world has seen? Tonight I will pray for the people who know and believe what this country has to offer, but I will also pray for the many people with hate in their hearts. I will pray that God will allow them to feel His peace and presence. Hopefully, they will be able to take a step back and realize what they are doing to America and her citizens. We the People need to lean into Him during these trying times."

America, this text from my daughter says it all. A gracious act of kindness. But, that awkward feeling someone will be offended and challenge you. That is what our world has become. I applaud my daughter's thankfulness of military service and offer to assist a stranger who may need help, quick thinking and her immediate self devotion to not fall prey to the political vultures. I am also proud of her for the act of kindness, self reflection and charitable prayers to believers and non believers. As I have loved you, that love lives on. If this story doesn't bring a tear to your eyes nothing will. Her text says it all.

Always faithful and loyal.

v/ r

Dan

Dear America,

You ain't gonna believe this one America. I can hardly believe it myself. I haven't actually heard the video but I have heard of it. So, allegedly, this college professor was taped in class and made a statement to the effect that all 60,000,000 Trump voters should die. Well, there are about 63 million and change.

Based on the 2016 election. That would be a lot of dead people lying around. Okay. Seriously, how can a college professor even think about saying that in class. Is it because some of our educational institutions are not educating, but indoctrinating. How brazen is that statement she said. Damn it man. I think the FBI should look into this and question her, her family, her associates and her friends. She might just be a Domestic Terrorist. Wishing death to 60 million people is pretty out there in my simple way of thinking. Is she actually wishing for the genocide of a group of people whose political ideologies are different than hers? Pretty serious stuff. But this type of rhetoric is what is brought to the table nowadays. The party of tolerance. Really ain't tolerant. The party of Democracy. Really ain't. The party of rebuilding America. Really ain't. The Dems have slid so far left they just might fall into Communist China. Heck fire they would be right at home. I personally don't have any social media accounts but I have heard this professor is really getting roasted for her comments. One I heard about was, "Even if all 60 million Trump supporters die, we can still vote. The deceased Democrats have been doing it for years." Person who said that is unknown and the quote ain't exact. Credit to the unknown. But it was a very clever response to this shallow minded professor who wished death to millions. If We the People aren't getting the message by now that the Transformation of you, America, is full steam ahead, they should get it now and understand the situation. Now more than ever We the People who cherish this country and believe in this American Ideal and experiment in human freedoms need to vote out the Socialist/Communist agenda being touted by the Dems. Our educational institutions should be teaching our children to be better citizens, teaching our children to be more socially acceptable, teaching critical thinking, teaching American history, the good and the bad, and preparing them to have a chance to pursue happiness and success. Educating them. Not indoctrinating our children to hate you America. Not to hate our history. Rather understand it. Teaching is not a platform to express their political views. For that is an unforgivable sin. Our youth need to learn. Research. Digest. Ask questions. And form their own conclusions by experiencing all views and opinions. After all, they are young Americans. So hear this biased educators, your days of indoctrinating our youth may be coming to an end. You really ain't that smart. The bias has been exposed. Please teach our youth fairly and unbiased. To those educators who hate America, I say this. Teach yourselves to love America again. And if you cannot, then teach yourselves to be fair and unbiased. Stop robbing our youth of being able to make their own choices as Free Young Americans.

Always faithful and loyal.

    v/r
    Dan

Dear America,

    My ole friend. Writing to you helps me put things into perspective. Plus I find it comforting and reassuring. The general election is 3 weeks away. Early voting has already begun. I would be fibbing to you if I said I ain't worried. Matter of fact, I am down right scared over the outcome. The way I see it this election is about Socialism/communism vs Capitalism. Totalitarian rule vs Freedom. Control vs Liberties. At no time in my short life has an election been more important. I am so grateful to you and what this Republic has done for me and mine. The life of freedoms and liberties we have enjoyed. Although at times it was difficult and we did without, there was always this " You can do anything in America because you have the right to pursue happiness." My family and I kept plugging away and believing that hard work and perseverance would someday lift the burdens. I never gave up on you, America. I only hope others will believe and see what could be available if they only believed and put in the effort. Nothing is free. I believe that. I was raised that way. Do not to expect a free ride. I think life is better that way. Earn it through tenacity, grit and sacrifice. So when you reach your mountain top it is so much more refreshing. And if you don't, then rejoice in your efforts and accept the outcome. I know the confidence in the American idea is dwindling. But it can once again imbed itself in the hearts and minds of your citizens. Won't be easy. Just need to keep picking away at it until everyone sees the value in being an American. You are never out of the fight. Deep down inside of each and every human is the will to survive and succeed. You just have to find it. America is the land of opportunity. We believed that once. We can believe it again. Don't let these power hungry politicians persuade you otherwise. Their flowery words are hollow and mean nothing in real life. They embellish almost everything to frighten you. They distort the truth to lead you into their web of broken promises and false hope. I would ask all Americans, please believe in America again. We can do this as a Republic. Rebuke the lies, the deceit and deflection of the Liberals. Believe in our Constitution, Declaration of Independence, The Bill of Rights and America. Stand up for America, because America has never forsaken you. Only power hungry politicians have left you behind once the votes are tallied. Remember these words, the Government is where your dreams go to die. America is where you and you alone can make your dreams come true.

Always faithful and loyal.

    v/r
    Dan

Dear America,

My oldest and dearest friend. This will be my last letter until after the Presidential election. Your Republic, our American way of life, our Freedoms/Liberties as we know them hang in the balance of this election's outcome. I firmly believe that. No matter the result, my lovely wife, my great children, my super grandchildren, will be here by my side waving the Flag. The sun will come up and go down. I will get up every morning and be thankful I am on the right side of the ground below me. I will take that early morning breath of fresh air and shake those old tired bones and sore joints and move along. Then I know, I live to enjoy. another day. I swore an oath and by cracky I intend to support you, America, as long as I can walk or crawl. Remember The Patriots Pledge? I do. You have been through so much, but this, my Ole Friend, may be your bumpiest road. Fear not, there are more We the People who believe. It ain't over yet. Let's see how things shake out. Until then get some rest. We might need you for the hard uphill battle. Oh yeah, Pray everything will be okay. I stand at the ready by your side, to Keep this America Idea and experiment in human Freedom moving forward. You will have my unwavering loyalty and support. My wife and I will keep Old Glory flying for you.

Always faithful and loyal.

    v/r
    Dan

Dear America,

I sure miss writing to you. Our/Your Republic is a mess. Hopefully after the election I will have good news. Until then, rest up and be ready. We the People just might need you.

Always faithful and loyal.

v/r
Dan

Dear America,

I'm back. As I mentioned earlier I would not write until after the election. I think it is over. But there seems to be some concern over alleged wrong doings and possibly those who gamed the system. Appears there are a few anomalies in this voting cycle that should be looked into. Like Gore, Trump deserves his 30 days or so to look into those states that may have taken advantage of an unprecedented election voting system. I don't mean the absentee voting, that has been around a long time. I am talking about the mail in part. I for one never liked the look or smell of that. Nothing tied the ballot to the envelope. You would think the bar code on the envelope would be on the ballot. And the whole verifying signatures was bogus. I hope the politicians get this figured out before the next election. Can't have this as the norm or we will become a third world developing nation in regards to elections. Our Founding Fathers must be livid at how this election was conducted. You have read this before from me America, the Patriots Pledge, where we pledge to respect other view points. That being said the Left can learn something here. If Biden holds on and is the President, then he is the President, period. Our President. We don't have to like it, but that's how it is. Now the Left would shout and scream if Trump won, " He is not my President". Lesson in tolerance my Leftist. Who is really the tolerant ones? But of course they are still calling all those who voted for Trump racists. And there was even talk from an elected official, a self proclaimed socialists, to keep Trump voters social media information archived. And some have vowed to punish Trump supporters. How Communist is that. How dare they even think that as elected officials. Brazen little boogers. They are out of the closet now. Tell me America, how can the divide ever close if one side thinks the other is racists and one side thinks the other is socialists. I do not have that answer. All I can say is we will be watching President Biden, if, after the Electoral College is ratified in his favor, to see if he stays moderate. At some point he has to answer the mail from the far left. Otherwise they will revolt. That's what happens when you have too many boxes to cater to. We will be watching to see if this so called transformation actually gains traction. And we will be watching to ensure our Bill of Rights are not infringed upon any further. So, President Biden the career politician, said he would be President of all Americans. We will see and we will call him out on that promise if not kept. America, there are many who did not like President Trump, the non-politician, but he kept his promises and fought for Americans. We the People who believe in you America will keep watch and be ready to vote out those who stray from the America we love. We keep our promises too and support you. Hang in there Ole Friend we got your six.

Always faithful and loyal,

    v/r
    Dan

www.ingramcontent.com/pod-product-compliance
Lightning Source LLC
LaVergne TN
LVHW091602060526
838200LV00036B/966